"It takes a top-notch historian to separate myth from fact. On the historic 50th anniversary of the birth control pill, Elaine Tyler May reminds us that modern contraception has not been a destabilizing force, as so many fear-mongers would have us believe. To the contrary, it has served as a powerful agent of change in the lives of married women liberated to balance work and family and to realize their full potential as human beings. By helping to elevate the status of women, birth control has promoted prosperity and well-being in America and around the world."

—Ellen Chesler,
author of *Woman of Valor: Margaret Sanger and the Birth Control Movement in America*

"Before the iPod, before email, before personal computers even, the technology that truly changed the country was one little pill. Elaine Tyler May explores everything from population control to *Playboy*, libido to liberation, in this fascinating look at how the birth control pill has affected Americans at work and play since its inception in 1960. May's eye for colorful anecdotes and cultural iconography makes this a delightful journey. Women who remember when the pill was approved by the FDA will rejoice in this hindsight view of how it influenced the personal and the political, while a new generation will feel deeply grateful for the rights and liberties that they've taken for granted. This is history for people who are serious about sex."

—Courtney E. Martin,
author of *Perfect Girls, Starving Daughters: The Frightening New Normalcy of Hating Your Body* and Editor at Feministing.com

AMERICA
AND
THE PILL

AMERICA
AND
THE PILL

A History of Promise, Peril, and Liberation

ELAINE TYLER MAY

A Member of the Perseus Books Group
New York

Published by
Basic Books, A Member of the Perseus Books Group
387 Park Avenue South
New York, NY 10016

Books published by Basic Books are available at special discounts
for bulk purchases in the United States by corporations, institutions,
and other organizations. For more information, please contact
the Special Markets Department at the Perseus Books Group,
2300 Chestnut Street, Suite 200, Philadelphia, PA 19103,
or call (800) 810-4145, ext. 5000, or e-mail
special.markets@perseusbooks.com.

Designed by Brent Wilcox

Library of Congress Cataloging-in-Publication Data
May, Elaine Tyler.
America and the pill : a history of promise, peril, and
liberation / Elaine Tyler May.
     p.   cm.
ISBN 978-0-465-01152-0 (alk. paper)
   1. Birth control—United States—History.   2. Oral
contraceptives—Social aspects—United States—History.
3. Women—United States—Social conditions—20th century.
I. Title.
HQ766.5.U5.M39 2010
363.9'60973—dc22
                                        2009046957

10 9 8 7 6 5 4 3 2 1

In memory of my parents,
Edward T. Tyler and Lillian B. Tyler,
Birth Control Pioneers

CONTENTS

Introduction

*If [an oral contraceptive] could be discovered soon,
the H-bomb need never fall. . . . [It would be] the
greatest aid ever discovered to the happiness and
security of individual families—indeed to mankind. . . . The greatest menace to world peace and
decent standards of life today is not atomic energy
but sexual energy.*

John Rock,
clinical researcher of the
oral contraceptive, 1954[1]

It was the spring of 1960. The U.S. Food and Drug Administration had just approved the oral contraceptive for marketing. The pill's arrival marked the culmination of years of
development and testing and heralded a new era in the long
history of birth control. For the first time, a method of contraception separated birth control technology from the act of sexual intercourse and was nearly 100 percent effective. Women

wasted no time demanding prescriptions—a surprise to doctors, who normally told their patients what to take, rather than the other way around.[2] Within two years of its approval, 1.2 million American women were taking the pill every day. By 1964 the pill was the most popular contraceptive in the country, used by more than 6.5 million married women and untold numbers of unmarried women.[3] But "the pill," as it quickly came to be known, was more than simply a convenient and reliable method of preventing pregnancy. For its advocates, developers, manufacturers, and users, the pill promised to solve the problems of the world.

In 1960, those problems seemed daunting. The nation was in the midst of cold war with the Soviet Union, locked in a battle for the hearts and minds—and markets and political alliances—of peoples around the world. Former colonies were gaining their independence, and the two superpowers vied for their allegiance. American officials feared that communism might take hold in the developing world as a result of widespread poverty, due in part to the rapidly rising global population. They also foresaw that overpopulation could lead to human misery, unrest, violence, and war.

At home, the nation was in the midst of the baby boom. Couples married young and had children quickly. Yet American women were growing restless. They were eager for a reliable contraceptive that would free them from constant childbearing so they could take advantage of new opportunities opening up for women outside the home. At the same time, the sexual revolution was churning just below the surface of domestic tranquillity. Despite the taboo against premarital intercourse and the widespread celebration of marriage and family, the trend toward sexual activity without wedlock had already begun. A youth culture was emerging that would challenge many of the social, political, and sexual norms of the past, and the feminist movement was on the horizon. In 1960, when the Food and Drug Administration (FDA) approved the pill, the forces swirling around its arrival clashed in thunderous clamor.

While some observers and commentators feared that the pill would wreak havoc on morals and sexual behavior, others claimed that it would cure the social, sexual, and political ills of the day. In keeping with the military metaphors that permeated life in the early cold war era, many saw the pill as a "magic bullet" that would avert the explosion of the "population bomb." By reducing the population, it would alleviate the conditions of poverty and unrest that might lead developing nations to embrace communism, and instead promote the growth of markets for consumer goods and the embrace of capitalism. The pill would also bolster the "nuclear" family in the nuclear age with its promise of marital bliss. By freeing married couples from fears of unwanted pregnancy, it would foster planned and happy families—the key to social order. Medical and pharmaceutical promoters of the oral contraceptive often cast it as the means to this end, with success marked by the achievement of national and global transformation.

Curiously, the pill's most vocal advocates were relatively quiet regarding the impact of oral contraceptives on those who would take them every day: women themselves. With the exception of Margaret Sanger and Katharine McCormick, two elderly activists in the women's rights movement who were responsible for the development of the pill in the 1950s, few of the pill's earliest advocates saw its potential to liberate women. Women, however, saw it as precisely that. When the birth control pill arrived on the market, it unleashed a contraceptive revolution. For the first time, women had access to an effective form of birth control that did not require men's cooperation or even their knowledge.

The pill was indeed revolutionary, but it was not the first reliable birth control method. For centuries, women as well as men had found ways to suppress fertility and avoid pregnancy. Prior to the arrival of the pill, men controlled two of the most widely used methods: condoms and withdrawal. Women employed a variety of barrier methods, such as sponges, pessaries, and the diaphragm. Abortion was widely used as a method of birth control, and surgical sterilization was also available. Potions and remedies of various sorts appeared on the market in the nineteenth and early twentieth centuries. Sold as a means to "regulate" the menstrual cycle, they often came with bold warnings that their use might prevent pregnancy or cause miscarriage. Women rushed to buy these products to achieve the dire consequences advertised on the product's packaging.

In the 1950s, pharmaceutical companies gained FDA approval for a hormonal compound that would cure menstrual irregularities by temporarily suppressing ovulation. Realizing its contraceptive potential, half a million American women suddenly sought medication for "menstrual irregularity," a condition rarely treated prior to the availability of the ovulation-suppressing remedy. In 1960, the FDA approved this compound as the first oral contraceptive, Enovid, manufactured by the G. D. Searle pharmaceutical company.

Having full control over contraception was a mixed blessing for women, because it relieved men of any responsibility for preventing pregnancy, leaving the burden entirely on the female partner. At the same time, the pill brought a third party into the equation: the doctor. Although the diaphragm, too, involved medical intervention for the initial fitting, there was no need to see a doctor thereafter. The pill, however, required regular checkups and monitoring. A doctor had to authorize every prescription and every refill. At first, few women complained about this intervention. As medical experts, doctors carried tremendous prestige and respect in the decades following World War II, when science and medicine gained unprecedented stature. This was the era of the expert, and experts seemed to be solving problems right and left. Americans were well primed to place their faith in scientists, doctors, and the pill to solve global, social, and personal problems. Advances in medicine yielded penicillin and the polio vaccine, tranquilizers to calm Americans' nerves in an era of anxiety, and now the pill, which promised to make unwanted pregnancy a thing of the past.

But the pill also empowered women to make demands on their physicians—initially by asking for prescriptions and later by insisting on more information and safer oral contraceptives. Within a few years of its FDA approval, as side effects and dangers became apparent, women came to realize that although the pill might solve some of their problems, it could also create many more. As the feminist movement gained momentum, women's health advocates protested pharmaceutical companies' indifference to their well-being and demanded government action.

Women were not the only ones affected by the pill. For every woman taking or contemplating the pill, there was at least one man involved. Men responded to the pill primarily through media spokesmen, who took up the social, sexual, and moral implications of oral contraceptives. Although some men found it liberating to be free of the possibility of impregnating their partners, others found the power and autonomy it gave to women threatening to their masculine egos. Meanwhile, researchers tried to develop a pill for men—an effort that continues to this day.

As it turned out, the pill did not solve all the problems of the world. It did not eradicate poverty, nor did it eliminate unwanted pregnancies or guarantee happy marriages. But it became a major player in many of the most dramatic and contentious issues of the last half of the twentieth century: the quest for reproductive rights; challenges to the authority of medical, pharmaceutical, religious, and political institutions; changing sexual mores and behaviors; reevaluation of foreign policy and foreign aid; and women's emancipation. The pill did not cause any of these developments or determine their outcome, but it was a hot-button issue for debate amid the social and cultural upheaval of the time. Eventually, the pill took its place not as the miracle drug that would save the world, but as an important tool in women's efforts to achieve control over their lives.

Although the developers of the pill came from many different countries and its impact was felt globally, in many ways the story of the pill is an American story. Two American women, Margaret Sanger and Katharine McCormick, succeeded in getting the pill developed; it was mostly American researchers and physicians who created and tested it, primarily American pharmaceutical companies that initially marketed it, and American women, overwhelmingly, who consumed it.

Millions of women have their own personal stories about the pill, and some of them are contained in the pages that follow. Through an Internet survey, I received e-mails from hundreds of women and a few men. Respondents of all ages, backgrounds, religions, and sexual orientations told me their stories. They wrote of the impact of the pill not only on their bodies and their fertility, but also on their lives. They help provide the personal dimension to the history of the pill during its first half century.[4]

I TOO HAVE A STORY. THE PILL HAS SPECIAL RESONANCE for me because my parents were involved in its early development and distribution. I was twelve years old in 1960, when the pill came on the market. I probably knew more about oral contraceptives than most girls my age. Dinner-table conversation often revolved around my father's work as a clinical researcher testing the pill in his private practice, or my mother's efforts to establish birth control clinics in Los Angeles where the pill was offered free of charge and my father served as medical director. I remember the press swarming around my father's office, and I watched when he was interviewed. Would the pill make women promiscuous? No, he insisted. Like most of the pill's advocates, he disapproved of premarital sex and believed that single women who engaged in sex would do so with or without the pill. But he hoped the pill would prevent unwanted pregnancy.

I tagged along to medical meetings where the pill was a hot topic. I remember debates and controversies about side effects and risks, and my father's frustration at the lack of a perfect control group to compare the health of pill-taking and non-pill-taking women over a long period of time. People I knew as my father's friends and colleagues I would later read about as birth control pill pioneers.

I was also a "human guinea pig" for the pill. In the early 1970s, after I was married, I asked my father what pill I should take. He suggested that I join the clinical trial of a low-dose pill being tested at the time. I dutifully showed up for the frequent medical checkups and lab tests required of study participants. My medical records are among the thousands used to document the safety and effectiveness of the low-dose pill.

Although I knew my father was involved in research on the pill, until I began working on this book I had no idea that he played a key role in the FDA approval process. As I read recent work by scholars in the field of medical history, I discovered that my father's caution and uncertainty about the safety of the pill delayed its approval, to the annoyance and consternation of the oral contraceptive pioneers John Rock and Gregory Pincus. The FDA refused to approve the pill for market until my father gave the green light. Prompted to write this book because the fiftieth anniversary of the pill's approval was approaching, I was astonished to find my father at the center of that momentous event.[5]

So while my interest in the pill predates my life as a historian, I now understand the events that swirled around me in a new way. This study of the pill also dovetails with my long interest in women's history, particularly the relationship between private life and public policies. Questions of politics, gender, sexuality, fertility, and reproduction have all been central to my work—and are all central to the history of the pill. As the fiftieth anniversary of the pill's FDA approval approached, I decided to investigate its impact on our lives and our world.

I wish I had been able to interview my parents for this project, to gain their wisdom and insights, hear their stories, and have them read and comment on my drafts. But they are no longer with us, so the best I can do is to dedicate this book to their memory, with gratitude for the work they did on behalf of women's reproductive freedom.

1

Mothers of Invention

You wined me and dined me
When I was your girl
Promised if I'd be your wife
You'd show me the world
But all I've seen of this old world
Is a bed and a doctor bill
I'm tearin' down your brooder house
'Cause now I've got the pill
All these years I've stayed at home
While you had all your fun
And every year that's gone by
Another baby's come
There's a-gonna be some changes made
Right here on nursery hill
You've set this chicken your last time
'Cause now I've got the pill
This old maternity dress I've got
Is goin' in the garbage
The clothes I'm wearin' from now on

Won't take up so much yardage
Miniskirts, hot pants, and a few little fancy frills
Yeah I'm makin' up for all those years
Since I've got the pill
I'm tired of all your crowin'
How you and your hens play
While holdin' a couple in my arms
Another's on the way
This chicken's done tore up her nest
And I'm ready to make a deal
And ya can't afford to turn it down
'Cause you know I've got the pill
This incubator is overused
Because you've kept it filled
The feelin' good comes easy now
Since I've got the pill
It's gettin' dark it's roostin' time
Tonight's too good to be real
Oh but daddy don't you worry none
'Cause mama's got the pill
Oh daddy don't you worry none
'Cause mama's got the pill

Loretta Lynn
The Pill, 1975[1]

C ountry singer Loretta Lynn's rebellious anthem, the first popular tribute to the pill in music, tells the story of a woman whose dreams of marital bliss and adventure have been thwarted by constant childbearing. Resentful of her husband whose prenuptial promises went unfulfilled as she stayed home to tend to their brood, she declares her independence with sexy clothes and good times, thanks to the pill. But she does not abandon her mate. The last verse of the song hints at one of the pill's initial promises: satisfying marital sex. She tells her man that without worries about pregnancy "the feelin' good comes easy now" and invites him to a night of pleasure. She lets him know that the pill has positive benefits for him as well as for her: "Oh daddy don't you worry none / 'Cause mama's got the pill."

Loretta Lynn's song articulates the hopes for liberation the pill promised to women. She sang to and for women who saw the pill as providing freedom from the fear of pregnancy and offering the opportunity to enjoy their sexuality with their chosen mates. Like the vast majority of women who took the pill, the song's protagonist was married, and her dreams had been displaced by the birth of one baby after another. The pill offered her a chance once again to reach for her dreams.

By the time Loretta Lynn belted out her hit song in 1975, the pill had been on the market for fifteen years and millions of women were taking oral contraceptives every day. As Lynn's lyrics suggest, the story of the pill is a story about women. That fact may seem obvious to twenty-first-century readers. But when the pill first came on the market in 1960, few people imagined how powerful a force for women's emancipation it would become. The scientists and medical researchers involved in the pill's development hailed it as a miracle drug that would solve the global problem of overpopulation, thereby reducing poverty and human misery, especially in the developing world. They also saw the pill as the key to family planning, allowing couples to space their children, enjoy marital sex, and achieve domestic harmony. But women had other hopes for the pill, and it was their dreams that brought the pill to fruition and made it a powerful tool for change.

The story of the pill is shrouded in myths and misconceptions, particularly as regards the central role women played in its development. The names most closely associated with the pill's arrival are Carl Djerassi, who first discovered how to synthesize the hormone progesterone from Mexican yams; Gregory Pincus, the scientist who discovered how to use this synthetic progesterone, known as progestin, to inhibit ovulation; and John Rock, the physician who first tested the pill on human subjects and became its most visible champion. But these men did not initially set out to develop an oral contraceptive. Many of the developers of the pill were trying to find a cure for infertility, an effort that led them to contraceptive research.

In spite of competing claims of paternity, there was no "Father of the Pill." In fact, the pill had two mothers: birth control pioneer Margaret Sanger and the wealthy women's rights activist Katharine McCormick. Both were in their seventies at the time they began their collaboration. As lifelong feminists, they had participated in decades of activism on behalf of women's rights. They knew that women could not achieve full equality unless they had control over their reproductive lives. Although the two would never benefit from the pill themselves, it was Sanger and McCormick's tireless efforts that made the pill possible.

THE WORK OF SANGER AND MCCORMICK BUILT UPON centuries of women's efforts to control their fertility. In the United States, by the nineteenth century contraceptive practices were widespread and reasonably effective, resulting in a dramatic decline in the birthrate. In 1800, American women had an average of eight children. By 1900 that number had declined by half. Nineteenth-century women controlled their fertility through several different means: late marriage or no marriage, sexual restraint, coitus interruptus, barrier methods such as the condom, pessaries (suppositories inserted in the vagina to kill sperm or block its entry into the uterus), and abortion. Abortion was common and generally accepted until "quickening," the point at which a woman can start to feel the movement of the fetus, which usually occurs about four months into a pregnancy.[2]

Among the experiments in fertility control were those adopted by utopian and religious communities that sought to alter sex, gender, and family arrangements as well as reproductive practices. The Shakers did away with sex altogether; Mormons established polygyny; and the Oneida Perfectionists turned to "group marriage" in which the community's leader gave certain couples, selected according to eugenic principles, permission to procreate, and everyone else was allowed to have sex with whomever they wished as long as they practiced "male continence"—intercourse without ejaculation. Women's rights leaders also called for new approaches to sex, marriage, and reproduction. They promoted "voluntary motherhood," which would give women the right to decide if and when to have children. Some radical activists went further. "Free love" advocates like Victoria Woodhull and anarchists like Emma Goldman sought to liberate women from the shackles of marriage altogether.[3]

It was not until the late nineteenth century that policies limiting access to birth control and abortion began to develop, promoted largely by the emerging medical profession, whose mostly male practitioners sought to take control over the process of pregnancy and birth from midwives and lay healers. At that time, zealous campaigners against all forms of behavior they considered to be immoral took aim at contraception, calling it a "vice." The most aggressive was Anthony Comstock, a United States Postal Inspector and longtime vice crusader who began a campaign against all forms of birth control. In 1873 a federal law named for Comstock equated birth control with pornography and prohibited all contraceptive information and devices from being sent via the U.S. mail. The Comstock Law restricted access, but it did not prevent women from obtaining birth control. Women shared information with each other by word of mouth and found ways to transport devices without using the mail system. They also mounted challenges to the law that eroded its prohibitions. Advertisements for contraceptives used euphemisms such as "effective for female disorders," or contained warnings that "special care should be taken not to use the remedy after certain exposure has taken place, as its use would almost certainly prevent conception." In spite of such efforts to get around the Comstock Law, it remained in effect for more than half a century.[4]

As the women's rights movement gained momentum in the early twentieth century, activists demanded not only the vote but also equality in marriage, access to divorce, and the right to engage in or refuse sex and reproduction. The birth control movement emerged as part of this wide-ranging feminist agenda. Both Sanger and McCormick began their careers as women's rights activists during this time. At that point, birth control advocates promoted contraception as a radical idea linked to political change as well as personal emancipation.[5] Margaret Sanger and Katharine McCormick were part of this movement for radical change. Their dream for a contraceptive that would be entirely controlled by women emerged at this time. Sanger, a feisty socialist and militant feminist, came from a working-class background. Her radicalism drew on her roots. Writing in *The Woman Rebel*, a periodical she began publishing in 1914, she declared, "The working class can use direct action by refusing to supply the market with children to be exploited, by refusing to populate the earth with slaves."[6] Sanger coined the term "birth control" in 1915, and within a few years she asserted her leadership of the movement that would be her driving passion for the rest of her life.[7]

Sanger's woman-centered approach to contraception emerged directly from her personal experience. The sixth of eleven children born to Irish Catholic immigrant parents, she watched her mother weaken and die at the age of fifty. She blamed her mother's premature death on constant childbearing and lack of access to contraceptives. Working as a nurse, Sanger also encountered many women who became sick and died from illegal abortions or, like her mother, simply having too many children.

She also considered contraception necessary to ease fears of pregnancy so that women could enjoy sex. Margaret Sanger expressed her hopes for a "magic pill" to prevent pregnancy as early as 1912 when she was thirty-three years old.[8]

But Sanger's advocacy of birth control was thwarted by legal restrictions, especially the Comstock Law. Along with many other birth controllers, Sanger challenged the law in several acts of civil disobedience. During these years, at least twenty birth control activists went to prison on federal charges.[9] Sanger was first arrested in 1914 for promoting contraceptives in *The Woman Rebel*. Rather than face incarceration, she fled the country and spent the next two years in Europe. While she was away, her husband, William Sanger, was arrested for distributing "Family Limitation," a birth control pamphlet written by his wife. In a raucous courtroom scene, William Sanger confronted Anthony Comstock as the assembled crowd of Sanger's supporters—including a number of well-known socialists and anarchists—hooted, jeered, and shouted at Comstock and the judge until the rowdy spectators were removed from the courtroom. The judge convicted Sanger, declaring the pamphlet "immoral and indecent," and scolded, "Such persons as you who circulate such pamphlets are a menace to society. There are too many now who believe it is a crime to have children. If some of the women who are going around and advocating equal suffrage would go around and advocate women having children they would do a greater service."[10]

In 1916, Margaret Sanger returned to face her own trial, and went to prison for opening the first birth control clinic in the United States. Although her clinic was in violation of the law, her strategy was to work with doctors to lend her movement legitimacy. That strategy served her well in the long run. After her release, she challenged the law that prohibited the distribution of birth control information. Although her conviction was upheld on appeal in 1918, Judge Frederick E. Crane provided for a medical exception to the law that allowed physicians to offer contraceptive advice to married women for the "cure and prevention of disease." With this new loophole in the system, Sanger promoted the establishment of birth control clinics across the country to be staffed by physicians who could legally provide contraceptive information and devices. She challenged the law again in 1936 in the U.S. Circuit Court of Appeals. The case, *United States v. One Package*, allowed physicians to send contraceptives through the mail, effectively removing birth control from Comstock Law prohibitions.

To promote her crusade for birth control, Sanger compromised her initial radical socialist principles. In the 1920s, she forged ties with medical professionals, including promoters of eugenics, whose conservative politics embraced immigration restriction and advocacy of laws for the sterilization of the "unfit." She continued to work closely with these physicians as a way to gain legitimacy for the birth control movement. By 1935, when most birth control advocates were strong New Deal liberals, Sanger attacked Franklin Roosevelt for his ambivalence about birth control using eugenic arguments: "As long as the procreative instinct is allowed to run reckless riot through our social structure . . . as long as the New Deal and our paternalistic Administration refuse to recognize [the danger this poses], grandiose schemes for security may eventually turn into subsidies for the perpetuation of the irresponsible classes of society."[11]

By this time, the birth control movement had already gained considerable mainstream acceptance and had lost its radical edge. With the lifting of Comstock Law restrictions and the need to limit family size during the Great Depression, the number of birth control clinics in the nation grew from fifty-five in 1930 to more than eight hundred in 1942. In that year, the Birth Control Federation of America changed its name to the Planned Parenthood Federation of America (PPFA), signaling a major shift in the movement's direction. New goals included strengthening the family by making it possible to plan the timing and spacing of children and by liberating female sexuality in marriage, leading to happier couples and greater domestic contentment. Improvements in barrier methods, including the condom and the diaphragm, increased the effectiveness of these contraceptives.[12]

By the 1950s, the promise of women's emancipation faded as the goal of family harmony came to the fore. Contraception was no longer part of a wide-ranging feminist agenda. In fact, Sanger had become an outspoken advocate of population control and family planning. As she wrote to Katharine McCormick, "I consider that the world and almost our civilization for the next twenty-five years, is going to depend upon a simple, cheap, safe, contraceptive to be used in poverty stricken slums, jungles, and among the most ignorant people. I believe that now, immediately there should be national sterilization for certain dysgenic types of our population who are being encouraged to breed and would die out were the government not feeding them."[13] She still promoted the idea of a simple contraceptive that would be entirely controlled by women, but held to the belief that the medical profession should regulate and dispense contraceptives. A birth control pill, which she first imagined in 1912, remained her ultimate goal.

That dream became a reality as a result of Sanger's partnership with Katharine Dexter McCormick. Brilliant, dedicated, and passionate, McCormick was a courageous lifelong activist on behalf of women's rights. The two ardent feminists first met in Boston in 1917 at one of Sanger's lectures, and they quickly became friends. In contrast to Sanger's modest economic circumstances, Katharine Dexter was born into wealth. The child of a successful Chicago lawyer, Katharine had advantages few young women of her generation enjoyed. She was the second woman to graduate from the Massachusetts Institute of Technology (MIT). Later she became an active alumna who pushed the school to admit more women. When it became clear that female students at MIT needed an appropriate living space, she funded the construction of a women's dorm. Challenging the status quo at every turn, she hosted dinners for MIT's female students and lectured them on the importance of birth control—a particularly bold move at a time when contraception was not only socially taboo but also illegal in Massachusetts.[14]

In 1904, the year she graduated from college, Katharine Dexter married Stanley McCormick, son of Cyrus McCormick, inventor of the reaper and founder of International Harvester Company. Soon after their marriage Stanley was diagnosed with schizophrenia. As the disease progressed, Katharine gained control of their vast estate and devoted her energies and resources to finding a cure for the illness. At the same time, she remained active in the movement for women's rights, a cause that attracted many educated young women of her generation. She became vice president and treasurer of the National American Women's Suffrage Association and worked toward gaining women the right to vote. She also became involved in the birth control movement. In the 1920s, she smuggled diaphragms into the United States from Europe to supply Sanger's clinics. McCormick's willingness to defy both custom and law served her well when she teamed up with Sanger to promote the development of the oral contraceptive pill.

In 1950, three years after her husband's death, McCormick contacted Sanger to ask how she could provide financial support for research on contraception. At the time, contraceptive research was considered a disreputable business. Pharmaceutical companies as well as the federal government refused to invest in it. In fact, throughout the 1950s, neither the National Science Foundation nor the National Institutes of Health provided any funds for contraceptive research.[15] In 1959, President Dwight D. Eisenhower proclaimed, "I cannot imagine anything more emphatically a subject that is not a proper political or government activity or function or responsibility. . . . The government will not, so long as I am here, have a positive political doctrine in its program that has to do with the problem of birth control. That's not our business."[16] Such resistance did nothing to deter McCormick and Sanger. Although the Planned Parenthood Federation under Sanger's leadership contributed small amounts of funding to early research, it was ultimately Katharine McCormick who bankrolled the development of the pill.[17]

Sanger and McCormick teamed up and began looking for someone who would carry their idea into a laboratory. They continued to insist on the need for a contraceptive that would be entirely managed by the women who used it. As strong proponents of women's right to control their own fertility, they believed it was essential that women have access to contraceptives that did not depend on men's cooperation.

THE FIRST TASK FACING THE TWO WOMEN WAS TO find someone to conduct the research. They set their sights on Gregory Pincus, a scientist with a somewhat tarnished reputation. In the 1930s, while he was an assistant professor at Harvard, Pincus engineered the first rabbit embryo in his lab. His research provided the foundation for in vitro fertilization, which decades later would become a standard treatment for infertility. Although his achievement was scientifically important, the media unleashed a storm of moral condemnation. Pincus was accused of sinister designs. He was even compared to the villain in Aldous Huxley's *Brave New World* who bred babies in test tubes. A 1937 article in *Collier's* magazine claimed that Pincus was creating a world of "Amazons" where "woman would be self-sufficient; man's value zero." At Harvard, the bad publicity apparently weighed more heavily than Pincus's significant research. In 1936, Harvard cited his work as one of the greatest scientific achievements in its history—nevertheless, it denied him tenure.[18]

Relieved to be free from the constraints of academia, Pincus teamed up with Hudson Hoagland, a Clarkson University biologist, and together they founded the Worcester Foundation for

Experimental Biology. Although he had to scramble for funding, Pincus continued his research. Meanwhile, other scientists pursued investigations that would contribute to the development of the pill. Chemists Carl Djerassi and Russell Marker synthesized progesterone from a plant source, the Mexican yam. Although its contraceptive potential was not immediately evident, Pincus and his colleague Min-Chueh Chang tested the synthetic hormone, called progestin, for its ability to inhibit ovulation.[19]

At the Worcester Foundation, Pincus was experimenting with hormonal compounds with the hope of finding a treatment for infertility. Sanger first met Pincus through Dr. Abraham Stone, the director of her Research Bureau in New York. In 1951, Sanger granted Pincus $5,100 from PPFA to begin working on a hormonal contraceptive. Sanger then approached McCormick with a more ambitious plan to finance Pincus's research specifically to develop an oral contraceptive. McCormick liked what she saw at the Worcester facility and pledged to provide Pincus $10,000 per year. She herself had a scientific background, having studied biology at MIT, and personally oversaw the research as well as providing financial support. McCormick ended up contributing more than $2 million to the pill project over the years— the equivalent of about $12 million in year 2000 dollars.[20]

The collaborators brought to the project a tremendous faith in the possibility of science to solve the world's problems and bring about a better future. One of the first women trained as a biologist, McCormick was both enthusiastic and impatient as she monitored every stage of research. As a nurse, Sanger had long believed that science held the key to contraception and to women's emancipation. As early as the 1920s she had proclaimed, "Science must make woman the owner, the mistress of herself. Science, the only possible savior of mankind, must put it in the power of woman to decide for herself whether she will or will not become a mother." Pincus, brash and confident, was full of optimism about the possibility of an oral contraceptive. As he set to work on the task, he announced to his wife, "Everything is possible in science."[21] The flamboyant Djerassi claimed the pill's invention for himself, as the title of his book, *This Man's Pill*, makes clear.[22]

The combined efforts of these and other individuals working in various settings and capacities led to the discovery of the synthetic hormonal compound that suppressed ovulation. Pincus tested the compound on laboratory animals, but he couldn't conduct any clinical trials on humans. For this, the collaborators turned to Harvard-trained obstetrician and gynecologist John Rock, who was the director of Brookline's Reproductive Study Center. Rock and Pincus were both involved in research for treatments for infertility. Reproductive medicine was an expanding field in the 1950s. Infertile couples struggled in the midst of the baby boom, when it seemed as though everyone was procreating. Many clinical researchers who became involved in the development of the pill also sought cures for infertility. These physicians were interested in family planning. As one explained: "Every child should be a wanted child. Those who want them should be able to have them; those who don't should be able to prevent them."[23]

John Rock was among the physicians who worked on both fertility and contraception. Like Sanger and McCormick, Rock had a powerful independent streak that led him to defy religious, legal, and cultural taboos. The grandson of an Irish immigrant tailor and son of a liquor store owner, Rock grew up with a spirit of adventure and risk taking. In high school he won a scholarship to travel in South America, and he began his work life on a banana plantation in Guatemala. Rebelling against his boss in Guatemala and then against his father, who wanted him to become a businessman, Rock entered Harvard College and pursued a career in medicine. He grew up true to his Catholic faith but with a strong belief that his conscience should be his most important guide in life.[24]

Rock became one of the pioneering physicians in the field of reproductive medicine, working on both infertility and contraception. A practicing Catholic and a social conservative, he believed that in certain circumstances birth control was medically necessary, but only when there were particular health reasons to avoid pregnancy. Highly critical of routine use of birth control, he held "no brief for those young or even older husbands and wives who for no good reason refuse to bear as many children as they can properly rear and as society can profitably engross."[25]

But Rock took issue with the Catholic Church's prohibition against birth control, because it prevented physicians from acting in what they believed to be their patients' best interests. In the 1940s, he taught students at the Harvard Medical School how to fit patients with diaphragms—a bold move for a Catholic doctor in a state that outlawed the distribution of birth control information and devices. He advocated the lifting of legal restrictions that hindered physicians from providing patients with contraceptives. Later, he clashed openly with the Church, arguing that the pill was consistent with Catholic precepts. Rock insisted that it was not an "artificial" means of birth control because the hormones in oral contraceptives mimicked those that occurred naturally in pregnancy.[26]

Rock agreed to work with Pincus to test the potential for the hormone progesterone to inhibit ovulation in humans. Now all they needed was the essential ingredient: women who would volunteer for the studies. Rock found sixty volunteers. Some of the women who joined the clinical trials were infertility patients at the Free Hospital for Women; other volunteers were nurses at the Worcester State Hospital. The complicated procedure included daily basal temperature readings, vaginal smears, and urine collection as well as monthly endometrial biopsies. The results were promising: The drug apparently inhibited ovulation. But there were problems with the study. The numbers were too small, and only half of the women complied with the rigorous protocol. The challenge was to find a large group of volunteers who would be motivated to comply.

Katharine McCormick was frustrated by the difficulty of finding an adequate pool of volunteers. "The headache of the tests is the cooperation necessary from the women patients. I really do not know how it is obtained at all—for it is onerous—it really is—and requires intelligent, persistent attention for weeks."[27] She was eager to begin a major clinical trial but daunted by the challenge of finding women willing to participate.

Lacking access to volunteers, researchers turned to involuntary subjects. In one of the most disturbing episodes in the development of the pill, Pincus forced fifteen psychiatric patients at the Worcester State Hospital to participate in trials that would afford them no benefit. Unlike the women in Rock's earlier study, most of whom were infertile and eager to test the pill's potential to temporarily suppress ovulation, thus possibly stimulating the ovaries when the drug was withdrawn, the psychiatric inmates were neither at risk of pregnancy nor hoping to become pregnant. Experimental programs involving coercion were used to test other drugs as well at the time, before professional standards prohibited such practices. Nevertheless, because the pill was tested on physically healthy women who had nothing to gain by participating in the study and possibly a great deal to lose in terms of unknown risks and side effects, serious ethical questions have been raised about these tests.[28]

Critics have long faulted doctors, scientists, and pharmaceutical companies for exposing women to dangerous tests of high-dose hormonal contraceptives. While there were certainly some clear cases of abuse and unethical practices, such as the coercive studies using psychiatric patients, the testing of the pill largely conformed to the standards of the day and often exceeded them. At the time there were few regulations in place for the testing of drugs. Compared to other countries, the United States had relatively stringent requirements for gaining government approval because of FDA regulations. But it was not until 1962 that doctors were required to inform patients if the drugs they prescribed were experimental. Standards of informed consent for the testing of drugs were in the distant future.[29]

Although progesterone and estrogen had been administered to women for decades to treat gynecological disorders and prevent miscarriages, finding a large enough volunteer group to test the contraceptive effectiveness of these hormones presented a major challenge. The laws against contraception in Massachusetts, where small initial trials had been conducted, ruled out that state as a site for a large study. John Rock had previously studied the pill for its "rebound effect" to encourage fertility, with the hope that after an infertile woman stopped taking the pill, she would then start ovulating and become pregnant. That research did not violate any laws. But Rock knew that if he tried to test the drug as a contraceptive, he could face criminal charges resulting in steep fines and imprisonment.

So the researchers considered several other possible sites for a study, within the United States as well as outside the country. Katharine McCormick worried about finding a stable population of willing and cooperative volunteers. "Human females are not easy to investigate as are rabbits in cages," she noted. She was concerned that if the women did not stay in one place to allow for adequate follow-up exams, or if they did not take the pills consistently, "the whole experiment has to begin over again—for scientific accuracy must be maintained or the resulting data are worthless."[30]

In 1956, Rock and Pincus finally decided to conduct the first large-scale clinical trials in Puerto Rico. The island appeared to be an ideal setting for several reasons: No laws prohibited contraception, and in fact, there was already an established network of sixty-seven birth control clinics on the island. With more than six hundred people per square mile, Puerto Rico was one of the most densely populated areas of the world. Impoverished women living in crowded, disease-ridden conditions were desperate for birth control. At the time, the only option available to them for reliable contraception was sterilization, which had been vigorously promoted and was widespread on the island, due in large measure to funding from the wealthy eugenicist Clarence Gamble, a longtime advocate of sterilization of the poor. Puerto Rican women wanted a nonsurgical, reversible, and effective means of preventing pregnancy. Women who volunteered for the studies were given pills containing 10 milligrams of progesterone and small amounts of estrogen, many times greater than the pills on the market today. But at the time researchers were uncertain whether lower doses of hormones would be effective, and they wanted to be sure that the pill they tested would prevent pregnancy.[31]

In Puerto Rico, two women conducted the on-site trials, Dr. Edris Rice-Wray and Dr. Adaline Satterthwaite. Rice-Wray, a faculty member at the Puerto Rico Medical School and director of the Public Health Department's Field Training Center for nurses, was medical director of the Puerto Rican Family Planning Association. Working with Pincus and Rock, she set up a research site in a suburb of San Juan. Satterthwaite, who like Rice-Wray was born and trained in the United States, established a trial site in Humacao, a rural area. The women they recruited were eager to participate. Already saddled with large families, many were in poor health and malnourished, longing for an effective yet reversible contraceptive. So many women volunteered that some sites resorted to waiting lists.

The developers of the pill were particularly concerned about its safety. They put in place elaborate precautions to monitor the health of the women who took part in the trials, such as frequent medical exams and lab tests. Study participants in impoverished areas received medical attention vastly superior to what was normally available to them. The researchers were particularly sensitive to the effects of the pill because it was intended for healthy women. It was not a drug to cure a disease, which could have been tested on patients who were already sick. By the standards of the day, the studies were scrupulously conducted.

But there were serious problems with the trials. The high doses of hormones caused side effects such as nausea, headaches, and dizziness. In 1956, Rice-Wray reported that 17 percent of the participants complained of these symptoms. Even though the 10-milligram pill "gives one hundred percent protection against pregnancy," she concluded that it caused "too many side reactions to be acceptable." Rice-Wray tried to convince Rock and Pincus to end the study because of these problems, but they considered these symptoms to be minor and dismissed her concerns. Pincus claimed that many of the women's symptoms were psychosomatic. He asserted, "Most of them happen because women expect them to happen." But the side effects were real and serious, prompting many women to drop out of the study.[32]

Although women continued to volunteer for the studies, the investigators faced considerable hostility from suspicious offi-cials and the media. Local newspapers published false reports that a "woman dressed as a nurse" was distributing "sterilizers" and that "Nordic whites" were using "the coloured races as 'guinea pigs.'" Priests and disapproving husbands also persuaded some women to drop out of the studies.[33] Eventually, Rice-Wray and Satterthwaite were both forced to resign their positions. Yet there is no evidence that the researchers intentionally put women at risk. Women volunteered freely and enthusiastically.[34]

The women of Puerto Rico were not the only ones taking part in testing the oral contraceptive. Rock, Pincus, and their colleagues conducted studies in Haiti, Massachusetts, and New York City as well. Other researchers were also testing the pill at sites inside and outside the United States, including Tennessee, Seattle, Chicago, Los Angeles, Mexico City, Hong Kong, Australia, Ceylon, Japan, and Britain. The data collected from these trials contributed to the development of the compound that eventually received approval for marketing. After the drug was cleared in 1957 for the treatment of various gynecological disorders, developers in the United States and Britain began the process of gaining permission to market the pill for use as a contraceptive.[35]

The approval process took place in several stages. The United States had a formal regulatory procedure; Britain did not. Nevertheless, Searle's product, known as Enovid in the United States and Enavid in Britain, came on the market in both countries in 1957 as a treatment for infertility and menstrual disorders. Three years later Searle submitted a request that Enovid be allowed for use as a contraceptive. British authorities refused to discuss or even monitor Enavid for contraceptive use, insisting that the issue was too politically and morally sensitive. In the United States, the 1938 Food, Drug, and Cosmetic Act defined a drug not simply as something intended to treat a disease, but as a product "affecting the structure or function of the body." Under that definition, all contraceptives fell under FDA jurisdiction.

Government officials tried to distance themselves from the social and moral implications of the oral contraceptive by concentrating exclusively on safety concerns. As the FDA Deputy Commissioner wrote to a U.S. senator, "Although we recognize the presence of moral issues, they do not come within the jurisdiction of the FDA. Our consideration has to be confined to safety for intended use."[36] At the time, the FDA was overwhelmed with thousands of requests for approval of new drugs, with only a few regulators on staff. The application to market Enovid as a contraceptive was assigned to Dr. Pasquale DeFelice, a young obstetric gynecologist who was still completing his residency. Because of his lack of experience and the paucity of medical experts available within the FDA, the agency relied heavily on the advice of outside medical practitioners. In February 1960, the FDA wrote to seventy-five physicians at leading medical schools around the country asking them to evaluate the safety of Enovid. Many responded positively, reporting that they had found the drug to be safe and effective for short-term use in treating gynecological problems. But those reports were largely irrelevant to the question of the pill's long-term use as a contraceptive.

A dissenting opinion came from Dr. Edward Tyler, head of the Planned Parenthood Clinic in Los Angeles and a clinical researcher who had treated nearly two hundred patients for menstrual problems and infertility using Enovid as well as other hormonal compounds. Tyler had serious reservations about the pill's safety. While John Rock was satisfied that the pill was safe and Gregory Pincus dismissed the side effects as mere nuisances, Tyler found that a significant number of his patients experienced abnormal bleeding, weight gain, swelling from fluid retention, and other problems. In 1958, he reported those concerns at a medical meeting and caught the attention of an FDA official in attendance. Because he had no vested interest in any particular formulation of the oral contraceptive, the FDA considered Tyler to be more neutral than Pincus or Rock, who had both tested and promoted Enovid.

Tyler's concerns slowed down the approval process, causing Rock and Pincus considerable annoyance and frustration. But the FDA would not grant approval as long as Tyler had misgivings. After carefully reviewing the responses to the questionnaire, an FDA official interviewed Tyler as a final step in the process. Tyler assured the official that his earlier concerns had been addressed, and that he was now convinced that Enovid was safe. Finally, on May 9, 1960, the FDA announced provisional approval of the pill and, on June 23, officially approved the 10-milligram dose of Enovid for daily use as a contraceptive. Because there were still concerns about its long-term safety, the FDA limited use of the pill to two consecutive years.[37]

Of course, John Rock, Gregory Pincus, Edward Tyler, and the scores of researchers involved in developing the oral contraceptive could not have brought the pill to market without the women who participated in its testing. Margaret Sanger and Katharine McCormick lived to see the fruits of their efforts. By the time they died—Margaret Sanger in 1966 at the age of eighty-six, Katharine McCormick the following year at age ninety-two— millions of women were "on the pill." Yet with the exception of Sanger and McCormick, the pill's most ardent advocates saw its potential not in terms of women's emancipation but rather as a miracle drug that would solve the problems of the world.

2

The Population Bomb

Today the population bomb threatens to create an explosion as disruptive and dangerous as the explosion of the atom, and with as much influence on prospects for progress or disaster, war or peace.

Hugh Moore,
The Population Bomb, 1954[1]

When the oral contraceptive arrived on the market, its champions claimed that the tiny pill promised to end human misery and eradicate the causes of war by controlling population. In meetings and conferences across the globe, experts met to address the "population bomb." At one such meeting, in the summer of 1965, hundreds of medical experts gathered in Bombay (now Mumbai) to discuss the problem of overpopulation. The site of the conference was not accidental. India, one of the most densely populated and impoverished nations in the world, was a telling backdrop, a living showcase of the need for population control. Participants included doctors from all over the world, and Indian physicians comprised the largest group in attendance. Between the Western male doctors wearing suits and the sari-clad female physicians from India, where reproductive medicine was the domain of women, the contrast could not have been more striking.

The most dramatic moment in the conference came when an American doctor made the claim that oral contraceptives would solve India's overpopulation troubles. With a theatrical flourish, he unfurled a roll of birth control pills like a streamer and tossed it into the packed auditorium. The assembled medical professionals watched as the plastic-wrapped promise of health and prosperity rose into the air and hovered above them for an instant before gently settling across attendees' laps. The presenter then declared that the pill offered the solution to world hunger and poverty. Even in small villages with little access to medical facilities and low levels of literacy, women could easily learn to take the pill every day and control their fertility. This simple tablet would bring an end to India's most pressing problems. His extravagant prediction was breathtaking.[2] As it turned out, it was also wrong. India, with a population spread across the country in remote villages lacking the medical personnel required to provide prescriptions and exams, was one of the countries most resistant to the pill.[3]

Nevertheless, many experts and leaders in the United States and around the world believed that overpopulation was a serious problem and that the pill could help resolve it. World population had nearly doubled between 1900 and 1960, from 1.6 billion to 3 billion. It would double again by the end of the century. The population bomb seemed to be exploding, unleashing unforeseen human misery. Many believed that finding a solution would bring peace, prosperity, and the good life to all. Cold warriors in the West saw overpopulation as a political problem: Impoverished people in overcrowded countries might be tempted to turn to communism.

Woven into this prediction was the same ambivalence about scientific progress that had greeted the atomic bomb. Science had discovered the huge destructive power of nuclear energy—now it had to figure out a way to turn it to good use. Similarly, scientific and medical discoveries had improved life expectancy so dramatically that the death rate had declined, but the birthrate had not. Science would now need to find a way to lower the birthrate. The pill promised to be the stealth weapon that would defuse the "population bomb" by limiting the size of "nuclear" families across the globe.

Both at home and abroad, population control generated considerable controversy. Advocates who agreed on the need for access to family planning services did not all agree on goals or methods. Some were motivated by humanitarian concerns, others hoped to achieve cold war political aims, and still others were primarily interested in social engineering and eugenics. In the United States, population controllers included conservatives who considered the children of poor people to be a burden on taxpayers, eugenicists who believed in curbing the fertility of the "unfit," and environmentalists who saw the nation's growing population as detrimental to the natural world and a drain on resources.

Some experts believed the pill was the perfect solution because of its effectiveness and simplicity. Others thought the pill wasn't suitable for use among poor people. They feared that needy, uneducated women would not be able to take it properly and consistently, or that it was too expensive and required too much medical monitoring to be useful in remote areas. Issues of cost and medical care were real concerns, but in clinics where the oral contraceptive was offered free or for a modest fee, poor women requested it and used it with the same success as more affluent women. Women made their own decisions according to the contraceptive options available to them.

WOMEN'S DESIRES FOR EFFECTIVE BIRTH CONTROL converged with population controllers' efforts at social engineering. These efforts gained tremendous momentum in the mid-twentieth century due to the era's rapid population growth and the political imperatives of the cold war. But population control has a history that dates back to the nineteenth century. The birth control movement emerged parallel to the population control movement, and although they did not always have the same aims, the two often intersected. Population control was not a concern of the early birth control pioneers. The radical beginnings of the movement were grounded in the quest for women's rights. Birth control advocates argued that women could never achieve equality unless they were able to control their own reproduction. This was the starting point for Emma Goldman, Katharine McCormick, Margaret Sanger, and other leaders of the movement. At the same time, they saw contraception as vital to alleviating the suffering of poor women burdened by constant childbearing. This impulse brought birth control into the eugenic conversation. Radicals were as likely to advocate policies that dovetailed with eugenics as conservatives, albeit for different reasons. While conservative eugenicists aimed to reduce the population of the "unfit," women's rights leaders hoped to improve the health and well-being of mothers and children. As Emma Goldman asserted, "Woman no longer wants to be a party to the production of a race of sickly, feeble, decrepit, wretched human beings. Instead she desires fewer and better children."[4]

Over time, the birth control movement, especially under Margaret Sanger's leadership, became more fully aligned with the population control effort. By the 1950s, when the birth control movement shifted to an emphasis on family planning, these currents converged. The two terms—family planning and population control—were often used interchangeably, but they did not mean the same thing. Family planning emphasized individual choice, whereas population control focused on large-scale reduction of fertility rates.[5]

These movements merged into a coherent public policy agenda that was first articulated during World War II. Initially, family planning was geared toward domestic needs, reflecting the rational, scientific approach to family life. By the time the United States entered the war, birth control clinics had proliferated around the country.[6] In 1942, when the Birth Control Federation of America changed its name to the Planned Parenthood Federation of America, it marked a change in the organization's direction fully in keeping with this new national focus. According to Abraham Stone, medical director of the Margaret Sanger Research Bureau, "Planned parenthood" signaled "the need for individual couples to plan their families and for nations to plan their populations." Sanger vigorously opposed the name change. She believed that "planning" weakened the woman-empowering message of "birth control." Nonetheless, she was overruled.[7]

Wartime brought new attention to rational preparations. Family planning experts urged contraception as a scientific approach to personal happiness as well as national security. One poster declared, "MODERN LIFE IS BASED ON CONTROL AND SCIENCE. We control the speed of our automobile. We control machines. We endeavor to control disease and death. Let us control the size of our family to ensure health and happiness." PPFA proclaimed, "A nation's strength does not depend upon armaments and manpower alone; it depends upon the contentment . . . of its people. To the extent that birth control contributes to the health and morale of our people, it makes them less receptive to subversive propaganda, more ready to defend our national system. . . . Victory cannot be won without planning." With rational family planning, "more healthy children will be born to maintain the kind of peace for which we fight." Margaret Sanger herself called for "national security through birth control."[8]

At the same time, the war gave rise to the first direct connections between the American birth control movement and population control abroad. Looking toward the postwar era, the PPFA became more concerned with the international implications of contraception, not only for poverty and political unrest, but in relation to healthy markets abroad. After the war, concern shifted to the dangers of overpopulation in developing countries, where the population was growing twice as fast as in the industrialized world.

Population control seemed a panacea for the world's ills. The movement included government officials and professionals from around the globe, but most of the leadership and funding came from the United States. Years before the pill became available, population control advocates saw contraception as the key to development, prosperity, and the success of democracy and capitalism in developing countries—and the best means to avoid war, famine, and the spread of communism. To that end, new organizations took shape. Margaret Sanger founded the International Planned Parenthood Federation (IPPF) in 1952. That same year, John D. Rockefeller III established the Population Council. He promoted progressive, noncoercive principles geared toward alleviating human suffering rather than reducing the population: "Our concern is for the quality of human life, not the quantity of human life."[9]

Observers and commentators had a wide range of perspectives on the dramatic rise in world population, but all seemed to agree that it was reaching crisis proportions. Humanitarians voiced concerns about increasing poverty and the plight of the poor, who would likely face starvation and disease. Less charitable were the cold warriors who worried that overpopulated poor countries would be drawn to communism and align with the Soviet Union, or that the large families in the developing world would be unable to afford American-made consumer goods, undermining the potential for vast foreign markets.

Not everyone shared these concerns. The Catholic Church remained staunchly opposed to population control efforts, and others continued to argue that contraception was not a matter for public policy. Anticommunist crusaders could also be found on both sides of the issue. Some argued that contraception and population control were essential to stop the spread of communism, but a smaller group, including Senator Joseph McCarthy, claimed that birth control was a communist plot to weaken the country and spread immorality.[10] Population alarmists, however, seemed to dominate the debate.

McCarthy's opposition notwithstanding, anticommunism fueled much of this alarm. The Hugh Moore Fund distributed a pamphlet, *The Population Bomb*, frequently reprinted through the 1950s and 1960s, claiming that there would be "300 million more mouths to feed in the world four years from now— most of them hungry. Hunger brings turmoil—and turmoil, as we have learned, creates the atmosphere in which the communists seek to conquer the earth."[11] Moore and his allies made it clear that they were not particularly concerned about human suffering: "We're not primarily interested in the sociological or humanitarian aspects of birth control. We *are* interested in the use . . . which the Communists make of hungry people in their drive to conquer the earth."[12]

While Moore's views were extreme, he was not alone. Popular magazines pumped up the volume with headlines that announced, "Surging Population—An 'Erupting Volcano,'" "An Overcrowded World?" "Asia's 'Boom' in Babies," "World Choice: Limit Population or Face Famine." Articles also highlighted the increasing American population, asking "Where Will U.S. Put 60 Million More People?" and "How the Population Boom Will Change America." Prophets of doom warned that "The Human Race Has, Maybe, Thirty-Five Years Left."[13]

In spite of the alarms raised by the media, the U.S. government was initially reluctant to fund birth control efforts at home or abroad. Worries about alienating the Catholic Church, added to the aura of illegality and immorality that still surrounded contraception, kept investment in population control efforts at low levels. By the mid-1960s, however, the tide had turned. The widespread acceptance and use of the pill, along with increasing concerns about world population, had made contraception a legitimate subject for national policy. President Lyndon Johnson placed population control at the center of his program for foreign aid as well as his domestic War on Poverty. The results were dramatic. Between 1965 and 1969 government funding for domestic family planning programs grew from $8.6 million to $56.3 million. During those same years, U.S. support for similar efforts in the developing world grew from $2.1 million to $131.7 million.[14] Even Dwight D. Eisenhower changed his mind. In the mid-1960s he admitted, "Once as President, I thought and said that birth control was not the business of our federal government. The facts changed my mind. . . . Governments must act. . . . Failure would limit the expectations of future generations to abject poverty and suffering and bring down upon us history's condemnation."[15]

Eisenhower's change of heart indicates the extent to which expert and official opinion had accepted the imperative of population control. As Edward Stockwell warned in his 1968 book *Population and People*, "Regardless of whether or not the 'population bomb' represents a greater threat to the peace and security of mankind than the hydrogen bomb . . . the inescapable fact is that the rapid and accelerating rate of population growth in recent years has created an extremely dangerous situation in many parts of the world."[16]

Far more influential than Stockwell's book was Paul Ehrlich's 1968 best seller, *The Population Bomb*. Ehrlich warned that within a decade "hundreds of millions of people are going to starve to death" and predicted that a nuclear war would be fought over resources before the end of the twentieth century unless poverty in the developing world could be alleviated. But unlike the humanitarians who called for population control, Ehrlich's warnings were tinged with disdain for the poor. He predicted that armies of poor people would "attempt to overwhelm us in order to get what they consider to be their fair share."[17] Ehrlich clearly believed that *we* deserve our fair share, but *they* do not. Ehrlich did not represent the views of all advocates of population control. But he had a huge following. In the midst of social and political turmoil of the late 1960s, Ehrlich's warnings struck a chord. His book sold 2 million copies by 1974.

Ehrlich was one of the founders of Zero Population Growth (ZPG), a movement that took shape in 1968.[18] In the spring of 1970, *Life* magazine ran a feature on ZPG, noting that the movement challenged the United States to stop growing. While cold war imperatives led some population planners to focus on the developing world, an entirely different group began advocating population control at home, motivated by environmental concerns. Gaining support among the young, especially on college campuses, ZPG advocates called on Americans to limit the size of their families to two children as a way to keep the population stable. According to *Life*, ZPG called for abortion reform, legalization of birth control, and changes in welfare regulations and tax exemptions for children—a collection of policy initiatives that spanned the political spectrum.

The tactics of ZPG included street theater and other forms of grassroots activism. At the University of Pennsylvania, women students organized a "Lysistrata Day," complete with toga costumes, in which they pledged "to avoid contact with men—for a day, at least." (In Aristophanes' play, the women refused sex until the men gave up war.) *Life* quoted Ehrlich, who had a vasectomy after fathering one child: "The mother of the year should be a sterilized woman with two adopted children." He warned that the "cancer of population growth . . . must be cut out." *Life* retorted, "A certain cold and dispassionate cast of mind is required in order to regard the birth of human life not as a joyous event but as the proliferation of some deadly malignancy."[19]

Although *Life* bristled at the tone of the ZPG advocates, many other observers agreed that the American birthrate had to be brought under control. Concerns about overpopulation in the United States differed from those expressed about the same phenomenon in the developing world. As the focus of concern in poor countries, the problems appeared dire: more poverty, starvation, disease, and political turmoil—leading to massive suffering as well as wars and possible communist takeover. By contrast, overpopulation in the United States and other Western countries might entail discomfort, psychological distress, crime, and social unrest. In 1970 *Ladies Home Journal* ran an article by British scientist Gordon Rattray Taylor arguing that overpopulation in cities creates stress that "scars our minds and bodies" and leads to higher rates of crime, disease, and mental disturbances. Taylor quoted Dr. Paul Leyhausen, "a leading German ethologist," who asserted, "What every normal man wants for himself and his family is a detached house in an adequate garden, with neighbors close enough to be found if needed, or if one feels like a social call, yet far enough away to be avoided at other times."[20] By these standards, only affluent suburbanites were "normal."

WHILE THE EXPERTS WHOSE THOUGHTS APPEARED in the *Ladies Home Journal* presumed that everyone could afford a single-family home in the suburbs if there was enough open space, others worried about the economic effects of overpopulation.[21] Some arguments for domestic population control carried explicitly racial overtones. An expert quoted in *Esquire* said that population growth in the United States will "greatly increase the magnitude of juvenile delinquency, exacerbate already dangerous race tensions, inundate the secondary schools and colleges . . . and further subvert the traditional American Government system. . . . In Washington ninety percent of the schoolchildren are Negro, in Manhattan seventy-five percent are Negro or Puerto Rican—indicating the future city population." Warning of high unemployment and frustration for urban blacks, the author predicted that "the crowd, or the mob, seems likely to reappear as a force in politics." Referring to the 1965 riots in the mostly black Watts neighborhood of Los Angeles, the author concluded ominously, "Watts was a prelude."[22]

While some feared the eruption of urban violence, others resented the cost to society of the high birthrate of the poor. Although the majority of poor people were white, minorities were overrepresented on welfare rolls. Opponents of the welfare state complained that taxpayers were supporting the children of the poor and wanted to curb their fertility. Some proponents of birth control for the poor, like eugenicist Clarence J. Gamble, encouraged inexpensive contraceptives as well as sterilization for poor women.[23] These efforts had eugenic and racial overtones both in the United States and overseas. Concerns about the proliferation of nonwhite people fueled public policies encouraging poor people of color to curb their fertility, sometimes coercing them to do so.

At the same time, contraception was "a great thing for poor folks," in the words of one African American woman. But poor women were rarely able to gain access to these technologies on their own terms.[24] Regardless of the motives of advocates, poor women took advantage of whatever contraceptive services were available to them. Some wanted sterilization; others resisted it. Some eagerly sought to be part of clinical trials of oral contraceptives; others rejected the idea of being "human guinea pigs." Proponents and activists often disagreed on which women should have access and what contraceptive options should be offered.[25]

Women of color were justifiably dubious of the motives of family planning advocates. Black women in particular had reasons to be distrustful after centuries of manipulation of their fertility, beginning with slave breeding. Well into the late twentieth century, black women were subjected to forced sterilizations. Nevertheless, many were as eager for birth control as their white counterparts. *Ebony* assured its readers that contraception helped parents "space babies to make them a blessing rather than a burden."[26] Tensions remained between the desire for access to contraception and suspicions of the motives of birth controllers.

Margaret Sanger exemplified this tension between choice and coercion. There is no doubt that her early radicalism faded in the service of more conservative and eugenic rationales for contraception, as the birth control movement shifted to a more mainstream focus on family planning.[27] But Sanger's interest in contraception for the poor characterized her efforts from the very beginning. In 1938, she turned her attention to a "Negro Project." The proposal stated, "The mass of Negroes, particularly in the South, still breed carelessly and disastrously, with the result that the increase among Negroes, even more than among whites, is from that portion of the population least intelligent and fit, and least able to rear children properly." For all the racist overtones of that statement, the words were not those of a white bigot: Sanger was quoting verbatim W. E. B. DuBois, the renowned African American civil rights leader. DuBois was concerned that among black Americans, those with the highest fertility rates had the fewest resources to provide well for their families. Without access to contraception, he argued, they would be doomed to live in poverty.[28]

Sanger wrote that her goal was "helping Negroes to control their birthrate, to reduce their high infant and maternal death rate, to maintain better standards of health and living for those already born, and to create better opportunities to help themselves, and to rise to their own heights through education and the principles of a democracy."[29] Many birth controllers shared Sanger's concerns. Although some were more interested in reducing the fertility of those they considered to be undesirable, coercive policies never took hold in the United States.

Yet when the pill arrived, some saw it as a potential tool of racist social engineers. In the late 1960s, male leaders of the Black Power movement charged that the pill promoted genocide, and they encouraged black women to refuse to take it. In 1967, a Black Power conference in Newark, New Jersey, organized by writer and activist Amiri Baraka,[30] passed a resolution denouncing birth control. Even mainstream organizations such as the NAACP and the Urban League backed away from their previous support of contraception. Marvin Dawes of the Florida NAACP asserted, "Our women need to produce more babies, not less . . . and until we comprise 30 to 35 percent of the population, we won't really be able to affect the power structure in this country."[31]

Black women, however, resisted such claims. Although they were aware that some white proponents of the birth control pill and other forms of contraception hoped to reduce the numbers of black babies, they wanted the pill and saw it as essential to their reproductive freedom. In 1970, writer and activist Toni Cade responded to the male Black Power leaders by asking, "What plans do you have for the care of me and the child?" Frances Beal, head of the Black Women's Liberation Committee of the Southern Nonviolent Coordinating Committee (SNCC), insisted, "Black women have the right and the responsibility to determine when it is in *the interest of the struggle to have children or not to have them and this right must not be relinquished to any* . . . to determine when it is in *her own best interests* to have children."[32]

The conflict between women and men in the movement went beyond rhetoric. In Pittsburgh, William "Bouie" Haden, leader of the United Movement for Progress, threatened to firebomb a clinic. In Cleveland, a family planning center in a black neighborhood burned to the ground after accusations of "black genocide." Meanwhile, black female leaders like Congresswoman Shirley Chisholm pushed for increased access to birth control. A 1970 study found that 80 percent of black women in Chicago approved of birth control and 75 percent were using contraception.[33]

Lack of access to reproductive health care remained a serious problem for poor women, whether black or white. A study by the Department of Health, Education, and Welfare (HEW) found that only 850,000 out of 5.3 million poor women in the United States received family planning services, and most of them were white. *The Nation* observed in 1969, "Caught in the middle is the indigent American woman who wishes to have the same freedom to choose sex without conception that her middle-class counterpart enjoys."[34]

Proponents of population control encountered ambivalent reactions from the people they hoped to reach. Women eagerly sought birth control wherever it was available. But their motives were *personal*. They used contraceptives to control their own fertility, not to control world population. Officials from governments at the receiving end of international family planning efforts did not necessarily agree that population control was the best way to reduce poverty. In 1974, when the world population reached 4 billion, the United Nations held a conference in Bucharest on population and development. Delegates from developing nations claimed that population control was an attempt to conceal the huge gap in wealth between rich and poor countries. They argued that the best contraceptive is development. Pointing to trends in Europe and North America, they noted that population growth slowed as a result of economic development and education.[35]

In spite of suspicions about Western motives, the most draconian efforts at population control were promoted not by American or other Western agencies but by governments in Asia. Some governments offered incentives such as money or transistor radios as rewards for sterilization, or provided "finder's fees" to anyone who brought a man to a vasectomy clinic. The Population Council and the Rockefeller Foundation opposed all such forms of coercion or financial incentives in family planning programs in developing countries. As Frank Notestein, Princeton demographer and former president of the Population Council, said in 1974: "Coercion or the perception of coercion will bring down a government before it brings down the birth rate." He was right. In 1977 Prime Minister Indira Gandhi of India was not returned to office in large part because of her imposition of mandatory family planning measures.[36] The most coercive measure to be officially enacted is China's "one child per couple" policy, instituted in 1979. At that time the population of China was growing by 20 million each year. Twenty years later China's fertility rate had dramatically declined.

But such coercive policies were rare. By the end of the twentieth century, most governments in the developing world provided birth control services to their citizens. Access to contraception alone did not reduce population growth. The most important factor in lowering the birth rate was the education of women. As women gained more rights, opportunities, and access to education, they were able to assert themselves more fully in their families and society and to take more control over their lives. Contraception was critical to women's emancipation in the developing world. Without the ability to control their fertility, women would not have been able to take advantage of new opportunities for employment and participation in public life.

Sheldon Segal of the Population Council criticized those who promoted contraceptive saturation programs: "They seemed to have a dogged concern for numbers rather than for people and their needs. . . . Women were seen as objects through which to implement population programs and policies."[37] Segal noted the direct correlation between female illiteracy and fertility rates, demonstrating that when women are educated they have more opportunities and motivation to limit the number of children they bear.[38] He said that if he had one dollar to spend on population control efforts, he would spend it on the education of women.[39]

The fertility rate declined dramatically in the last half of the twentieth century, even if the population did not. The World Health Organization estimated that in developing countries the average number of children per woman declined from 6.1 in 1970 to 3.9 in 1990. In the 1960s, fewer than 10 percent of couples in the developing world used birth control; by 2000 nearly 60 percent did.[40] The availability of the pill (as well as the IUD and other forms of contraception) had been critical both in emancipating women and in reducing the fertility rate. One could not have happened without the other.

AS IT TURNED OUT, THE PILL PLAYED A MINOR ROLE in curbing population growth. It did not live up to dramatic predictions that it would solve the problems of overpopulation, poverty, and hunger. Across the world, middle-class women were much more likely to use the pill than poor women. Population planners saw the pill as part of the solution, but not necessarily the most practical contraceptive for use among the poor. In fact, in the early 1960s, the pill was rarely used in population control programs. Many preferred the IUD, because it required only one visit to a clinic and could remain in place for years. Using the IUD, women did not need to remember to take a pill every day, nor did they need to see a doctor for prescription refills. The pill was one among several contraceptive options available to women who wanted to control their fertility, assuming they had the opportunities that made fertility control possible for them.

In many areas, access to birth control depended on foreign aid provided by Western countries. In the United States, after Eisenhower's initial refusal to consider contraception as part of public policy, John F. Kennedy, the nation's first Catholic president, supported family planning programs as part of foreign aid, as did every president who followed until the United Nations conference on population in Mexico City in 1984. At that time, President Ronald Reagan reversed the United States' position. This reversal of long-standing policy was a direct result of abortion politics within the United States. The U.S. delegation to Mexico City included the Conservative Party senator James Buckley of New York and Republican Allan Keyes, both ardent foes of abortion. At the conference they established what came to be known as the "Mexico City policy": a global gag rule that refused U.S. government support to any agency, American or foreign, that used its own funds to support abortion services, counseling, or referral, even though these services would be legal and no U.S. money was involved. Many clinics that provided contraceptives also offered abortion services. The Mexico City policy prohibited these facilities from receiving any U.S. funds for family planning, even if those funds would not be used for abortion-related services. The vast majority of Americans opposed Reagan's gag rule, favoring the inclusion of family planning information and supplies as part of foreign aid, and disapproved of withholding funds to health organizations that provided abortion services with non-U.S. funds.[41] Nevertheless, the rule prevailed through the Reagan years and the presidency of George H. W. Bush.

In 1993, five days after taking office, President Bill Clinton dropped the Mexico City policy. The following year, the United Nations sponsored a population conference in Cairo. The "Cairo Agenda" focused on issues of women's rights, including reproductive rights, "free of discrimination, coercion, and violence." In spite of widespread support for Clinton's policies and the Cairo Agenda, President George W. Bush restored the Reagan-era gag rule three days after he took office in 2001. One staunch anti-abortion physician told a television news reporter that "the United States has to stop all those abortions caused by contraceptives, like the pill and the IUD." Sheldon Segal, who worked for decades to make contraception available to women throughout the world, was "astonished" by the lack of scientific accuracy as well as the hostility to women's reproductive rights that supporters of the gag rule expressed. The official position of the United States had come full circle—from initial reluctance to strong promotion of foreign aid for contraceptive services, then to a policy that deprived women throughout the world of access to birth control because of ideological hostility to abortion rights. During the administration of President George W. Bush, funding for family planning programs, including contraceptive services within the United States, declined in favor of "abstinence only" programs, which have been proven to be unsuccessful. The Bush administration's refusal to support any "unnatural" forms of birth control severely diminished worldwide efforts to make contraceptives available to poor women, including methods that inhibit the spread of AIDS.[42]

On January 24, 2009, four days after taking office, President Barack Obama reversed the policy once again, lifting the gag rule. Politically, the pill has traveled a bumpy road. But politics has not stopped women the world over from using birth control. There is no question that access to safe and reliable contraception, including the pill, has shown major benefit to women's lives. Today, over 60 percent of the world's married women in their reproductive years use contraception, and 90 percent of them use the pill, the IUD, implants, or injectables.

Fertility rates changed not because of the efforts of experts and population planners, but because at last women could decide whether they wanted more or fewer children.[43] Of course, the extent to which women could exercise their contraceptive options depended upon many circumstances, public policies among them. But besides her own desires, the most significant influence on a woman's use of birth control was likely to be her sexual partner. To understand the role of the pill in women's lives, it is necessary to consider men.

3

Bedfellows

With my wife on the pill, any moment is the right moment for love. No plans. No calculation. Unpremeditated sex is marvelous! We are in love, and it seems the right way for people in love to have sex.

Unnamed man quoted in
Ladies Home Journal, 1969

Many wives feel sexually liberated by birth-control pills. But some husbands feel enslaved. It's as if their sense of maleness and self-esteem has been threatened.

Dr. Robert Kistner, 1969[1]

The birth control pill made it possible, for the first time ever, to separate contraception from the act of sexual intercourse. Women could take the pill with or without the approval of their sexual partners—even without their knowledge. For women, this could be enormously liberating and empowering.

Men also benefited from the pill. They no longer had to contend with the clumsy condom or the awkward withdrawal method. The pill offered men the additional advantage of more eager and responsive partners freed from the fear of pregnancy. Without devices, appliances, or interruptions, and assured that their sexual encounters would not result in pregnancy, couples could unleash their passions freely. Uninhibited sex was one of the pill's most potent promises. But as the quotes above suggest, the pill might lead to sexual bliss, or it might do just the opposite. Not all men shared the profound sense of relief and freedom the pill offered women.

Along with preventing pregnancy, the pill challenged deeply entrenched sexual codes and attitudes. For men, the pill promised to relieve the worries of unplanned pregnancy: the burden of another mouth to feed, the anguish of a partner facing an illegal abortion, or the pressure of a shotgun wedding. Yet it could also undermine a sense of masculine potency grounded in procreative power. For women, the pill's benefits were obvious: freedom from the fear of pregnancy, convenience, and total control over contraception. Women had the most to gain from the pill, and the most to lose without it.

Before the emergence of the second wave of feminism and the powerful movement for reproductive rights, women struggled to avoid the dangers of unwanted pregnancy. The stakes were highest for single women. The powerful punitive culture at mid-century came down especially hard on sexually active single women. Even if an unmarried woman avoided pregnancy, she risked a tarnished reputation. If she had the misfortune to become pregnant, she faced the dire options of rushed marriage, dangerous abortion, or the shame, ostracism, and burdens of unwed motherhood. Married women also felt cultural pressures in the midst of the celebration of domesticity and motherhood that reigned during the baby boom era. They tended to emphasize the pill's promise of family planning and marital happiness, keeping the liberating potential of contraception under the radar.[2]

Meanwhile, it was men—especially those who considered themselves among the cultural avant-garde—who led the public charge for sexual liberation. They hoped to break down the barriers of prudery and restraint but with little regard for the reproductive consequences, and even less interest in women's empowerment. Among the most visible and outspoken proponents of sexual freedom in the 1950s and early 1960s were the Beats, who publicly flaunted their defiance of all forms of sexual propriety, both heterosexual and homosexual. Although the Beats included some "chicks" in their circle, the culture of male bonding and adventure among them was notoriously sexist. The women, according to Beat memoirist Joyce Johnson, were minor characters.[3] The Beat philosophy of sexual freedom did not necessarily include women's right to use contraception, which would thwart men's procreative powers. Beat poet Richard Brautigan expressed this sentiment in his poem "The Pill Versus The Springhill Mine Disaster":

When you take your pill
it's like a mine disaster.
I think of all the people
lost inside of you.

The poem, dedicated to his girlfriend at the time, equates the pill with the 1958 mining disaster in Springhill, Nova Scotia, in which trapped miners died. His poem likens the pill not to liberation but to death.[4]

A LESS DISMAL VIEW OF THE PILL CAME FROM ANOTHER proponent of liberated manhood: Hugh Hefner, publisher of *Playboy* magazine. In the 1950s, Hefner created and promoted the ideal of the suave, urbane, unencumbered bachelor. He built his Playboy empire by offering men the trappings of the "good life" without its burdensome responsibilities. Hefner was an instant celebrity and his magazine became a source not only of soft porn for mainstream men but of wide-ranging discussion of controversial issues, including sex and birth control. The magazine reached an audience of a million readers a month and had a profound impact on popular visions of the good life. The Playboy ethic encouraged men to enjoy the sexual pleasures of attractive women without the chains of marriage, and to pursue the rewards of consumerism as single men in well-appointed "bachelor flats" rather than as husbands and fathers in appliance-laden suburban homes. Hefner's magazine offered tips on how to achieve this lifestyle, along with centerfold airbrushed photographs of nearly nude young female "bunnies" who seemed to promise sex without commitment. Hefner's "Playboy Philosophy" promoted sexual freedom primarily for men, with women depicted as eager and willing "playmates."[5]

Playboy advocated an ideal of sexually free and sophisticated bachelorhood that did not reflect the reality of most men's lives. But it did provide a fantasy that appealed to millions of male readers eager to imagine a respite from the burdens of breadwinning, parenting, and sexual monogamy.[6] At the same time, Hefner considered himself a feminist, and promoted *Playboy*—the magazine as well as the lifestyle—as in the vanguard of the sexual revolution. A political liberal, he favored most policies promoted by mainstream feminists, and he was an early proponent of reproductive rights. In the magazine, he called for legalized abortion as early as 1965. The Playboy Foundation contributed thousands of dollars to support abortion rights, provided funds for child care centers for working mothers, supported the controversial research on human sexuality conducted by William Masters and Virginia Johnson, and donated to the American Civil Liberties Union for women's rights. *Playboy* even had female readers. Helen Gurley Brown, author of the 1962 best seller *Sex and the Single Girl*, founded *Cosmopolitan* as a *Playboy* for women and praised Hefner for promoting the idea that "women really *are* . . . as interested in sex as men are, if not more so."[7]

Hefner's support of women's rights, however, was limited. He scoffed at critics who claimed that *Playboy*'s centerfolds objectified women. For all of Hefner's claims to support gender equality, his magazine was hardly the place to find it. Women's bodies were certainly portrayed in a positive light, but women's activity outside the bedroom was viewed with considerable suspicion. Between 1953 and 1963 *Playboy* featured three major articles by the noted misogynist Philip Wylie, who coined the term "Momism" during World War II to describe women who allegedly smothered their sons with misdirected and sublimated sexual energy, turning them into "sissies" and rendering them unfit for the masculine role of soldier. In 1962 *Playboy* examined this theme in a forum on the same topic, in which eight famous men offered their expertise on the matter.[8]

The panel of experts included eight white men and no women. Among them were noted writers, doctors, scholars, artists, and entertainers, nearly all of whom agreed that "womanization" was endangering America and eroding men's rightful place at the helm. Only Dr. Ernest Dichter saw women's equality as inevitable, promoted not only by career opportunities but also by contraception. He wrote, "Woman has become a partner in the biological sense, in the psychological sense, and also in the whole concept of family planning, professional activities. Womanization has taken place only to the extent that it has brought the modern woman up to par with the male—though there is still not 100 percent equality." Dichter then asserted that as women gain more equality, "it's going to be the male who will profit by it. He's going to have a partner rather than a little doll that he has to take care of, which gives him a feeling of superiority, but in an illusory fashion."[9]

In a rebuttal to Dichter, *Playboy*'s editors took Wylie's side in the argument, as did the hipster comedian Mort Sahl, who chimed in, "The happiest chicks—the ones who are *really* ready for marriage, in a sense—are the ones who don't try to run it and are junior partners. They have it all—by letting the guy do it all for them." The Freudian psychoanalyst Dr. Theodor Reik got to the bottom of the issue: "What is astonishing to me is that women, more and more, are taking over the active roles in sex, which was not so before. The men finally will resent it. They should. It is, so to speak, in their masculine capacity." In other words, with the exception of Dichter, who saw women's emerging partnership with men as a positive development and who linked family planning to professional development, these male advocates of sexual freedom wanted to be sure that women's sexuality would be liberated for men, but not for women themselves.[10]

In light of Hefner's support for women's reproductive rights, it is somewhat surprising that in its early years *Playboy* had little to say about contraception. From 1953 to 1959, in spite of the magazine's focus on sexual pleasure and its centerfold photos, there was not one mention of birth control. In fact, there is no serious attention to the consequences of the sexual activity that the magazine so vigorously promoted. Gradually, the issues of fatherhood and unwed pregnancy crept into the pages of *Playboy*, but largely through humor. Three cartoons published in the early 1960s illustrate *Playboy*'s ideas about fatherhood. In one, a nurse tells a "hipster" man in a hospital waiting room, "You're a daddy-o." Another depicts a nurse holding a baby as the new father unbuttons the nurse's uniform to reveal her ample breasts. The caption reads: "Just a moment, sir—you're overly excited. . . . " In a similar cartoon, a new father and his male buddy look through a nursery window at a nurse holding twins who appear as the woman's breasts. The new dad exclaims, "Not bad for a shot in the dark, eh, Frisby?!"[11]

The magazine's editorial cartoons continued to trivialize and discourage fatherhood. One depicted a couple in a primitive tropical setting with thatched hut and palm trees, surrounded by six children, as the wife reads a card: "Oh, my God! We've been invited to another fertility rite!" Another suggested the horrors of parenthood as a couple sipping tea looks up dreamily at an image of a monstrous giant baby hovering over them, drooling and with bulging eyes, as if about to devour them.[12]

Unwed motherhood also provided fodder for the magazine's ironic humor. Some cartoons depicted pregnant single women as brazen, such as the 1965 image of an expectant enlisted woman speaking to a military officer who has apparently just reminded her of the rules against sex with married military personnel: "Of *course* I know regulations, Larry—I'm not married." Others suggest that single pregnancy continued to be shameful. In one cartoon, a young pregnant woman sits at the desk of a doctor, who says, "Now then, Miss Frimley, suppose you tell me a little more about this 'friend of yours' who is in a bit of trouble. . . . "[13]

One of the more sympathetic and serious of this genre appeared in 1965, depicting a young couple strolling arm in arm down a tree-lined street with houses behind picket fences. They both carry schoolbooks and the young man wears an athletic letter sweater, suggesting they are in high school. Both look glum. The young man says, "'Too young to stay out late! . . . Too young to smoke or drink. . . . Too young to go steady! . . .' Gee, they're sure going to be surprised when they find out you're not too young to be pregnant!" Finally, in 1966, *Playboy* takes on the pill and single women directly in a cartoon depicting Old Mother Hubbard living in a shoe, surrounded by a mob of children. A young lady, presumably one of Hubbard's offspring, strolls off on the arm of a young man as her mother yells at her through the shoe window: "Did you remember to take your pill?"[14]

During the 1960s, *Playboy* became more political in its articles, taking on such topics as the cold war, the hydrogen bomb, and the civil rights movement. At this time, the magazine became an advocate for the pill as well as a major site for panel discussions and debates about sex and contraception aired in its articles and letters to the editor. In 1964, Hefner's regular editorial feature addressed the topic of "religion in a free society" and examined all the major religions' attitudes toward sexual morality. Hefner was particularly critical of the Catholic Church for its opposition to birth control, but he expressed optimism that the pill and the population explosion might revise the Church's position. His article sparked a flurry of letters to the editor. One writer clarified the Church's position by explaining the difference between various forms of birth control, articulating the circumstances in which the Church allows for contraception and even abortion (to save the woman's life). In response, *Playboy* stated that non-Catholics are often "baffled" by the distinction between "the 'naturalness' of rhythm and the artificiality of oral contraception" but went on to say that the Church can make whatever distinctions it wishes, as long as it did not impose its will on others through laws limiting access to birth control.[15]

Playboy also began a sustained criticism of the Catholic Church for its specific opposition to the pill. Writers advocated both contraception and legalized abortion as necessary for solving the problem of worldwide overpopulation. One letter to the editor criticized the arrest of a speaker at Boston

University who lectured on birth control and abortion. "Instead of being arrested, he deserves an award for public service."[16]

Hefner himself promoted access to the pill for single women and urged that facilities such as university health services provide prescriptions. He criticized a Cleveland court for finding a woman guilty of contributing to the delinquency of a minor for giving her underage daughter information on birth control. Hefner noted that the teen had already given birth to three illegitimate children and declared that the judge's verdict reflected "the severe and inhumane belief that the girl should be made to pay for her sin with pregnancy." He argued that giving the pill "to the girls who request them is in the best interests of the girls themselves, and that this, after all, should be the deciding factor."[17]

But Hefner's insistence that the "deciding factor" should be what is in "the best interests of the girls themselves" may have been a bit disingenuous. Soon, *Playboy* began insisting that women take the pill regardless of side effects or reservations, claiming that those who resisted the pill were neurotic, prudish, hostile to men, or unwilling to take responsibility for contraception. (There was no similar insistence, however, that men should take responsibility for contraception.)[18] In 1966 a woman wrote a letter to the editor complaining that *Playboy* considered the birth control pill "the panacea for the problem of unwanted pregnancies both inside and outside of marriage." She pointed out the unknown risks of long-term use and the side effects that some women find "so bad that they cannot take the pills." *Playboy* replied by suggesting that complaints of side effects were merely old wives' tales: "It's always a bit galling when a scientific discovery threatens a long-cherished religious or moral notion."[19]

Some letters to the editor appeared to be written by the editors themselves, in order to provide an opportunity to respond. One allegedly female writer asked, "I am told that birth-control pills bring on many of the discomforts found in early pregnancy: sore and swollen breasts, excessive appetite and weight gain and sometimes even morning sickness. Does *Playboy* have anything to say about these disadvantages?" It is unlikely that an anonymous woman from Long Beach, New Jersey, would write to *Playboy*, of all magazines, for advice about contraception. In their response, the editors quoted a psychiatrist who claimed, "Women will tolerate side effects . . . if they enjoy sexuality, do not perceive their husbands as being excessively sexually demanding and feel generally responsible for managing family planning."[20]

WITH EXPERTS PROVIDING LEGITIMACY FOR THEIR claims, the editors of *Playboy* embraced the pill as a key to sexual liberation and pleasure, especially for men. Other experts, however, claimed that men were not necessarily liberated when their sexual partners took the pill. Indeed, some authorities warned that men might experience negative side effects. According to a psychoanalyst writing in *Redbook*, many men "see their virility in terms of what they can do *to* women. A man like that used to be able to give his wife babies—lots of them—whether she wanted them or not. But the pills take this last bit of masculinity away from him."[21]

The noted psychotherapist Rollo May agreed: "Being able to get a woman pregnant is a much deeper proof of manhood than anything else our culture has to offer." Because women take the pill, "Men are withdrawing from sex. . . . Impotence is increasing. Men feel like drone bees."[22] Psychiatrist Andrew Ferber added to this dismal view of contemporary manhood: "The male libido depends on culture. In our culture, the ability of the man to procreate is perhaps irrevocably tied to sex drive." Sounding one note of optimism in this otherwise grim view, a male physician opined that it may be too late for today's middle-aged men, but younger men might be more receptive, because they are "tuned into the population problems and are minus some of their parents' sex hangups."[23]

Dr. Robert W. Kistner, the Harvard professor of obstetrics and gynecology quoted at the beginning of this chapter and a leading expert on the pill, wrote in *Ladies Home Journal* in 1969 that when the pill first became available, many expected husbands to rejoice because the pill would "liberate the act of love from the specter of pregnancy and release pent-up womanly passion. . . . These assumptions, unfortunately, may not be universally true." Kistner warned his female readers that some husbands may experience "frustration, worry, fear and occasionally impotence" when their wives take the pill and become more sexually eager. He explained that for some men, sexual arousal results from competition and conquest of a reluctant wife. Some of his female patients "complained that their husbands would become sexually aroused when they undressed before them, only to lose their desire if the wives assumed the dominant role in the sex act or became the least bit animalistic."[24]

Other experts echoed this concern. One noted that the typical overworked husband comes home "mentally and physically spent—in no mood to satisfy his newly libidinous, pill-taking wife." No longer the "virile attacker," he becomes the "docile partner rendering mere service to his peer—or at least he feels that way." Another described a woman who began taking the pill and "enjoyed her newfound sexual freedom almost to the point of nymphomania," causing her formerly virile husband to become hostile, surly, impotent, and violent.[25]

In a telling comparison, another doctor observed, "Woman power is just like black power, and it's going to have a similar impact. Faced by the growing public effectiveness and independence of women, men have traditionally reacted as if their masculinity were under attack. . . . American men are beginning to show a preference for demure, passive women. Perhaps the golden day of the shy Southern belle is due for revival." This physician suggested that black power threatened white privilege much as women's power threatened male privilege. According to this logic, white men were at risk of losing their sexual as well as racial dominance—and the pill was part of the problem.[26]

Sex educator Dr. Mary Calderone was not surprised by these responses, noting that the sexual effects of the pill could bring a woman "face to face with her own sexuality or that of her husband—a confrontation that often results in anxiety or panic on the part of the husband or wife." Ultimately, these experts offered a predictable solution to the problem of the pill's adverse effects on men: more experts. They suggested psychotherapy to help couples adjust to the impact of the pill on their sexual relationships.[27]

As these experts and advocates demonstrate, the pill altered the sexual dynamics between women and men. More than simply providing effective and convenient contraception, the pill disrupted power relations between the sexes. Whether the pill was a boon for men or a bust, millions of women took it anyway, and their sexual partners managed, happily or unhappily. The pill clearly revolutionized contraception. Whether or not it revolutionized sex is another matter.

4

The Sexual Revolution

The pill is obviously important to the sexual and the contraceptive revolutions, but it is not the opening bombshell of either one.

Gloria Steinem, 1962[1]

Everyone knows what The Pill is. It is a small object—yet its potential effect upon our society may be even more devastating than the nuclear bomb.

Pearl S. Buck, 1968[2]

The pill is a symbol of the sexual revolution of the 1960s, attached to the decade's utopian dreams—or dystopian fears—that sex was increasingly escaping its marital confines and exploding among the unwed. As the metaphors of warfare in the above quotes suggest, the oral contraceptive was one more weapon in the growing arsenal of the prevailing cold war culture. Heated controversies erupted over its impact on the nation's sexual behavior.[3] The apocalyptic foreboding of the noted writer Pearl S. Buck reflects worries at the time that the pill would destroy the nation's sexual mores and unravel the fabric of marriage and family, leading to social chaos. Feminist Gloria Steinem, on the other hand, saw the pill as contributing to the increasing autonomy of married and unmarried women as well as an important contribution to their sexual emancipation—but not the cause of either development.

In fact, we know very little about the pill's relationship to the sexual revolution. Although increasing numbers of unmarried women engaged in sex and some of them used the pill, the vast majority of women who rushed off to their doctors to obtain prescriptions for oral contraceptives were married. Single women faced many obstacles. Laws in several states prohibited doctors from prescribing the pill to them. Some single women lied about their marital status in order to get the pill; others found sympathetic doctors. A doctor working in Boston told Gloria Steinem in 1960 that he prescribed the diaphragm for anyone who asked, ignoring the Massachusetts law that prohibited the distribution of birth control information or devices: "I don't know a doctor who demands a marriage license before giving contraceptive advice or prescriptions. The law says 'health reasons' and leaves the interpretation up to our discretion. We proceed on the basis that unmarried women need medical contraceptive methods for their own and for society's health." One young single woman told Steinem that it was "simple" to get contraceptives. "Just go to a doctor and tell him you're getting married. I went through the whole bit, including a blood test, just to get a diaphragm."[4] Not all young women would consider that process "simple." But those who wanted birth control could usually find a way to get it.

Custom more than law stood in the way. If the only deterrent to sex for single women was fear of pregnancy, and if unmarried women had been champing at the bit for a safe, convenient, and effective method of contraception, both sexual intercourse and pill use among the unwed would have increased dramatically after the FDA approval in 1960. And if large numbers of sexually active single women had used it, there would have been a significant decline in abortions as well as out-of-wedlock births. But none of that happened. The availability of a particular technology rarely creates an immediate change in deeply held cultural values. The diaphragm, for example, had been available long before the pill, and although it was less convenient, it was almost as effective. But neither the diaphragm nor the pill sparked a major change in sexual behavior. In the 1960s, many other factors were involved in unleashing the sexual revolution.[5]

Polls taken at the time indicated that single women who were already sexually active were enthusiastic about the pill because it allowed them to enjoy sex more fully. But those who were not engaging in sex were not likely to do so simply because the pill was now available. As one doctor noted, "The pill does not make people decide to have sex. It is after they decide to have sex that they go get the pill." Nevertheless, the pill was part of a changing cultural environment that was gradually becoming more tolerant. A psychologist pointed out that a large part of the sexual revolution resulted not so much from changes in behavior as from "increased freedom to *talk* about that behavior—and to admit to it without apparent shame or guilt."[6]

Gloria Steinem noted an increasing public acceptance of sex and an emphasis on individual moral choices. With more young women becoming "self-motivated and autonomous . . . they are free to take sex, education, work and even marriage when and how they like." The pill, she believed, encouraged this trend, but didn't create it. She concluded that as women gained more independence, the availability of the pill would "speed American women, especially single women, toward the view that their sex practices are none of society's business."[7]

STEINEM'S OBSERVATIONS PROVED TO BE PRESCIENT. Women used the pill to further a trend that had been developing for several decades. The rise in sexual activity among single women in the 1960s appears dramatic not because it was historically unprecedented but because it was such a stark contrast to the 1950s—an aberrant decade marked by a widespread rush to the altar. The marriage rate skyrocketed as people wed at younger ages, creating the baby boom. In fact, 1957 marked the high point in births among teenagers, with nearly 10 percent of fifteen- to nineteen-year-old women having babies. But 85 percent of those young mothers were already married. By 1959, nearly half of American brides were younger than nineteen. Teen sex had undoubtedly increased during the 1950s, but young marriage was a substantial part of the equation.[8]

If the 1950s and 1960s are viewed in a longer historical context, changing patterns appear more evolutionary than revolutionary. The rate of premarital intercourse among American women who came of age in the 1920s was more than twice that of the previous generation. By the early 1950s, half of all American women had engaged in sex before marriage. The numbers increased rapidly in the late 1960s and even more dramatically in the 1970s. By the late 1980s, premarital sex was the norm for both women and men, with a majority of young women becoming sexually active by the age of nineteen.[9] There is no evidence that the pill's arrival in 1960 had any immediate impact on these trends. Two eras stand out as moments of dramatic change: the 1920s, when new dating customs gave young couples more privacy and sanctioned a greater degree of physical intimacy; and the late 1960s and 1970s, marked not only by changing behavior but also by a greater openness surrounding public discussions of sex. In both periods, sexual activity, including intercourse, increased among the unmarried.[10] And in both "sexual revolutions," effective contraception played a role, but not a causal one.

In addition to fostering intimacy among unwed couples, both revolutions liberated and encouraged marital sex. In the early twentieth century, increasing numbers of medical experts acknowledged that women as well as men had powerful sex drives, and that sexual fulfillment was equally important for husbands and wives. Romantics like Margaret Sanger saw birth control as contributing to the greater expression of female sexuality, which she saw in idealized, spiritual terms. In her 1926 sex manual, Sanger articulated her belief in the uplifting power of physical intimacy: "Sex-communion should be considered as a true union of souls, not merely a physical function for the momentary relief of the sexual organs. Unless the psychic and spiritual desires are fulfilled, the relationship has been woefully deficient and the participants degraded and dissatisfied. . . . The sexual embrace not only satisfies but elevates both participants. The physical demands are harnessed for the expression of love."[11] Sanger's words reflected the views of many sex reformers throughout the 1920s and 1930s.[12]

World War II created new opportunities for previously taboo sexual behavior among single men and women, especially among many "respectable" young women, who discovered sexual adventures amid the upheavals of wartime. At the same time, the war glorified marriage, home, and family as the American way of life for which the country's soldiers fought and died. During the war, in major Hollywood films such as *This Is the Army* and *Penny Serenade*, marriage and babies took center stage. When the war ended, much of the sexual activity unleashed during the war became enveloped in marriage, as young people focused their hopes for peacetime happiness on domestic bliss. The double standard, which had eased somewhat during the war, returned with a vengeance. For the next two decades, sex for women was contained largely within marriage, where happy families were expected to flow naturally from procreative intercourse.[13]

But the white picket fences surrounding these idyllic homes didn't contain the sexual desires of postwar couples. Within marriage, young wives faced more than two decades of fertility and worried about bearing and rearing too many children. Outside of marriage, the stakes were especially high for women. Young men faced little or no stigma for their sexual adventures—some dalliance on the way to manhood was expected, and men often boasted of their conquests. For women, shame and notoriety followed those who "went all the way." If "caught" with a pregnancy, a couple either married quickly under the scrutiny of family and friends or the unmarried woman had some hard choices to make. Many took the risk of an illegal abortion. The lucky ones found a private physician willing to provide a "therapeutic" abortion by claiming that continuing the pregnancy risked the life or health of the patient. But hospital policies were making that option more difficult by requiring a panel of doctors—not just the woman's physician—to agree that the procedure was medically necessary.[14] Others went through with their pregnancies at great personal cost. Young white women were often whisked away to homes for unwed mothers to give birth and put their babies up for adoption. Young black women—frequently denied access to white-only homes for unwed mothers—turned to their families to help raise their babies.[15]

Whether or not a pregnancy occurred, sex was risky for single women. Artists and writers explored the rigid sexual culture and its costs, especially for women. Two major American writers, Mary McCarthy and Philip Roth, took up this theme in their work. Mary McCarthy's 1954 short story, "Dottie Makes an Honest Woman of Herself," revolves around a sexually liberated college student's visit to a birth control clinic to be fitted for a diaphragm. The story caused a stir when it was published in *Partisan Review* and became a chapter in McCarthy's best-selling 1963 novel, *The Group*. Beginning with the words of Dottie's lover, "Get yourself a pessary," the narrative chronicles Dottie's search for both love and liberation, even though Dick, the man with whom she had lost her virginity, insists, "I don't love you, you know." As in many stories exploring the sexual dynamics of the era, Dottie is looking for love, and Dick is looking for sex.[16]

Like Mary McCarthy's story, Philip Roth's 1959 novel, *Goodbye Columbus*, also featured a diaphragm. The central plot—a romance between affluent Brenda Patimkin and Neil Klugman, her working-class boyfriend—turns on Brenda's bold decision to go to a clinic for a diaphragm and her mother's subsequent discovery of the device.[17] As in Mary McCarthy's story, the diaphragm leads to an unhappy ending. Neither Dottie nor Brenda finds true love; contraception does nothing to free them from shame, rejection, and heartbreak.

In a 2005 interview, Philip Roth reflected on the centrality of the diaphragm in his story. He recalled, "There was no legalized abortion [in 1959]; young men and young women were extremely concerned with not getting pregnant. . . . So it was a crucial issue, because there was no remedy short of something drastic, which was either marriage for very young people or an illegal abortion, which was quite terrifying, if one even knew how to go about doing it." When Brenda went to the Margaret Sanger Clinic for a diaphragm, "It may seem like a small thing now, but it really wasn't a small thing for Brenda, coming from her background, to do, it wasn't a small thing for [her boyfriend] to ask her to do. . . . Of course they're undone by that."[18] McCarthy and Roth, keen observers of sexual culture, made it clear that it would take more than effective birth control to transcend the taboo against unmarried sex, especially for women.

When the pill arrived in 1960, that taboo did not suddenly disappear. Looking back from the vantage point of 2007 with both hindsight and insight, the creators of the critically acclaimed AMC cable series *Mad Men* explored the sexual culture. Set in the early 1960s, the show profiles the world of a New York City advertising firm. In the first episode, a young secretary, learning from an experienced colleague that the way to get ahead in the job is through sex, goes to a physician to get a prescription for the pill. As the doctor gives the young single woman a pelvic examination, he lectures her about her sexual morals. He warns that he will stop prescribing the pill if she "abuses" it. He then hints that he's having an affair with her sexually adventurous colleague. The pill does not liberate the young secretary. In fact, she has sex with a married man at the firm and gets pregnant anyway.[19] The fictitious character in *Mad Men* suggests the perils that faced single women if they engaged in sex, with or without the pill.

UNQUESTIONABLY, THE PILL HAD ITS GREATEST IMPACT within marriage. The long-term benefits for married women were profound. The ability to plan and space the birth of children allowed them to take advantage of educational and professional opportunities that unexpected pregnancies precluded. They clamored for the pill, and after the FDA approved Enovid, millions rushed to their doctors for prescriptions.

For single women, the impact of the pill is less clear. Did access to the pill encourage women to have sexual intercourse when they might otherwise have refrained? How many sexually active young women actually used the pill? According to a college junior who surveyed two hundred college women for an article in *Mademoiselle*, "The pill will have no effect whatsoever on most women's desire for sex with one man within a permanent love relationship. It is within marriage that the pill should have its greatest impact, making sex a happier, freer act for those who choose to limit their families. . . . Anyone who expects a moral revolution will almost certainly be disappointed."[20] Although her article was geared to the magazine's teenage readers, her commentary reflected the sentiments of most college women at the time.

During the 1960s the birthrate declined, the marriage age rose, and sex among singles became more common and accepted. But attitudes were slow to change. A poll of 1,900 women students at the University of Kansas in 1964 revealed that the vast majority believed that premarital sex was wrong, even for engaged couples. Ninety-one percent disapproved of intercourse among couples who were not engaged to be married. It is likely, however, that more than 9 percent of these students were having sex with men they did not plan to marry, which suggests that they may have disapproved of their own behavior and felt guilty about it.[21]

After 1965, sexual intercourse among unmarried women began to increase, although rates for unmarried men showed no change since Kinsey's studies in the late 1940s. The double standard may have been eroding, but some sociologists questioned whether the slight changes in sexual behavior evident at the time could be considered a "revolution." The role of the pill was equally unclear.[22]

Nevertheless, sensational media coverage linked the pill to an upheaval in sexual behavior. *U.S. News & World Report* asked, "What is 'the pill' doing to the moral patterns of the nation?. . . . Is the pill regarded as a license for promiscuity? Can its availability to all women of childbearing age lead to sexual anarchy? Are old fears of the social stigma of illegitimacy about to become a thing of the past?"[23] Many people worried that women with sinister motives would claim to be on the pill when they were not, and would get pregnant on purpose to trap a man into marriage.[24]

Although liberals and conservatives alike disapproved of premarital sex, they differed on their assessment of the pill. Conservatives blamed it for unleashing the sexual revolution. Liberals argued that women who were "promiscuous" (a term never applied to men) would engage in sex whether or not the pill was available. They promoted the pill as a way to prevent unwanted pregnancies among sexually active young women.[25] Gregory Pincus, John Rock, and other pioneers insisted that the pill would not change the behavior of unmarried women. Rock noted that young people already knew how to use makeshift condoms: "Any high school kid can get other contraceptives and probably knows about Saran Wrap." Betraying his disdain for sexually active young single women, he quipped that contraceptives were readily available "for naughty little girls who want to use them."[26]

In January 1964, *Time* echoed Rock's disapproval in its cover story "SEX in the U.S.: Mores and Morality." Condemning the "cult of pop hedonism and phony sexual sophistication," *Time* blamed science, secularism, and the media. The magazine presented the pill as playing a role in all this—but not a major one, noting that in spite of available contraceptives, the rate of out-of-wedlock births continued to rise. Some young women did not use contraceptives because they "resent the planned, deliberate aspect; they think it 'nicer' to get carried away on the spur of the moment." Although the double standard persisted, the "old taboos are slowly beginning to disappear. . . . The long-standing cold war between men and women in the U.S. may be heading for a *détente*."[27]

But not all agreed that a sexual revolution was under way, or that the pill had anything to do with it. As late as 1968, *Science News* reported that in spite of the "floodtide of publicity over oral contraception and its moral impact," the pill had had little effect on the sexual behavior of unmarried men and women. Noting that for nearly a century effective contraceptive devices had been available to those who wanted to engage in sex and avoid pregnancy, the author claimed that "young people don't generally base their decisions about sexual behavior on contraception."[28]

Sociologist Ira Reiss, a leading expert on sexual behavior, suggested that changing cultural and religious values had a greater impact on sex among singles than the arrival of the pill. "Perhaps one or two percent of premarital sex incidents are due to the pill," he asserted, but offered no evidence for that speculation. In his exhaustive study of nearly 3,000 unmarried women and men, he asked dozens of questions about sexual practices but nothing at all about contraception. Nevertheless, Reiss argued against the idea that a sexual revolution was taking place. In 1968, he noted, 60 percent of female college students were virgins when they graduated, only a small change from the days before the pill was available. Clinical psychologist Ernst Prelinger agreed that the pill did not create a sexual revolution. He speculated that young single women were reluctant to use the pill because it "impairs the poetry of the experience," and they did not want to appear "always sexually ready." This reluctance helped to explain the high rate of unintended pregnancies in spite of the availability of the pill and other forms of birth control.[29]

When news reports suggested that the pill could be used to prevent pregnancy "the morning after" if taken in a large dose, one man wrote a letter to *Playboy* heralding the development as a means of avoiding the problem: "This . . . will mean that girls can safely say yes, without having to feel that their assent was premeditated. This will eliminate the guilt many now feel about taking the pill before they are sure it will be needed. What a relief it will be when there's a medication that does not offend the female's sensibility but safeguards her security." According to this man, a single woman who responsibly planned ahead for her sexual encounters would be plagued by "guilt," but with the promise of retroactive contraception a man need not worry about seducing an innocent and unprotected "girl," because she can take care of it after the fact.[30]

Whatever the reasons, large numbers of sexually active young women were not using birth control. A 1968 study of sex and pregnancy among teens found that few had access to family planning programs, that they used birth control inconsistently if at all, and that they experienced high rates of contraceptive failure. Three years later, a survey revealed that more than one fourth of teenage women were sexually active but very few of them used contraceptives consistently. The researchers concluded that when "sexual encounters are episodic and, perhaps, unanticipated, passion is apt to triumph over reason." As late as 1972, a national survey found that three-fourths of sexually active young single women rarely or never used contraception.[31]

CLEARLY, THE PILL DID NOT RESOLVE THE TENSIONS and confusions that confronted young women during the "sexual revolution." Responding to an Internet survey, Rebecca L looked back forty years to her college days and recalled, "I chose to have intercourse for the first time my junior year of college. It was 1968 and I was twenty-one. I began dating in junior high and was involved in kissing, making out etc. I grew up with parents who thought that dating was very important, but also emphasized the importance of virginity at all costs. I was immensely confused about where to draw lines and how to draw lines, about good girls and bad girls. This was a remarkably frequent conversation topic with both my mother and my father through high school and college, at their initiation." As with many of her peers, Rebecca's ideas began to change, but her parents' did not, which meant that even if she had no qualms about her sexual behavior she faced the prospect of her family's disapproval. "By 1968 I was very conscious of a change in sexual mores and I wanted to get on with it. I began to think that what was acceptable or not acceptable for a 'good girl' was arbitrary. My junior year I became involved with a man a few years older than me and we very quickly decided to get married. I don't remember much discussion about having sex or not. I was ready. I don't remember anything about birth control and I don't remember this sexual relationship being very pleasurable." The relationship did not end in marriage, but it left Rebecca with a venereal disease. Living at home for the summer, she saw her family doctor for medication, which her mother discovered. "I had a horrific confrontation with my mother who asked me if I was a virgin and I said 'I'm not and it was beautiful,' which it wasn't."

Soon, Rebecca was sexually involved with another man, whom she would later marry. Although the pill was available, she did not use it. "I very actively chose to be sexual, but I really was not quite sure how to go about getting birth control. It was not that I was unwilling to see myself as sexually active, or that I didn't want to acknowledge my interest in sex. I was just not enough in charge of my life, and I had the enormous struggle with my parents' huge disapproval and shame. On the one hand I really rejected it. On the other hand, I had internalized it."

Rebecca ended up pregnant, and had an abortion. "I literally never took a risk with birth control again in my life." Today Rebecca and her husband are still married, the parents of two young women. She told them her history and encouraged them to use birth control as soon as they became sexually active. Many women of Rebecca's generation did not want their children to suffer the shame, danger, and conflict they experienced when they were young.[32]

Eleanor S also became sexually active in college. She too planned to have sex but did not use birth control. As a college senior in 1969, tired of the virginity obsession that had been drilled into her by her parents, she was determined to have sex with the next man she dated. "I decided to have sex before I knew who the guy would be. So when I started dating Gordon, we began having sex. . . . No fireworks, that's for sure. But as I look back on it, I was surprisingly irresponsible, thinking that I wouldn't get pregnant because of the time it was in my cycle. I knew the rhythm method didn't work, but that was all I used." Like Rebecca's first sexual relationship, Eleanor's didn't last long. Soon after breaking up with Gordon she began dating Donald, the man she would eventually marry. "At that point I knew enough to get reliable birth control, and I wanted to go on the pill." But she was reluctant to ask her family doctor for fear of his disapproval, and didn't know where else to turn. "I was very lucky that I didn't get pregnant."[33]

Rebecca and Eleanor were both children of liberal parents (although they were clearly not very liberal about unmarried sex). They were both feminists. They made the decision to engage in sexual intercourse well before the encounter, not accidentally in the heat of the moment. And they did not feel guilty about their behavior. They could have gone on the pill, but they didn't. The sexual revolution was real for these young women—sex was happening all around them, everyone was talking about it, the young men they dated expected to have sex with them, and they wanted to be freed from the rigid codes of virginity. But they did not have the confidence or easy access to get the pill, and they did not feel empowered enough in their relationships to demand that their sexual partners take adequate precautions.

Indeed, Rebecca and Eleanor were representative of college women in the 1960s. The sexual revolution unfolded gradually on college campuses across the country. Disproportionate media attention to hippies, communes, and visible centers of the counterculture such as Haight-Ashbury gave a skewed impression of the changes that took place in the 1960s. On campuses in the nation's heartland like the University of Kansas (KU), students protested against rules governing their personal behavior, *in loco parentis* policies, and what they considered a lack of respect for their independent judgment and maturity. University students asserted their right to make their own decisions about sexual behavior and to have access to contraceptives, including the pill.[34]

As students protested school policies at universities across the country, debates raged about whether or not the pill should be available at campus health centers. A majority of 20,000 respondents to a 1967 *Good Housekeeping* poll disapproved of distributing birth control to unmarried women, citing moral objections.[35] Campus officials faced competing pressures from public opinion and student demands. At Brown University, the president came to the defense of a beleaguered health official who had prescribed the pill for two unmarried students over the age of twenty-one. A student journalist argued that college policies should be "geared to safety and efficiency and not to the ordering of the personal lives of its students, or to the legislating of chastity." Regardless of the rules and public opposition, it appeared that college women who wanted the pill could get it. The head of student health at the University of Chicago said many women got the pill from family doctors at home and brought their birth control to college. "Or they borrow from each other or use the prescription of a married sister or they put on an engagement ring and get them as part of preparation for marriage. It's not a very formidable task to obtain the pills."

A West Coast doctor agreed: "There is certainly a lot of Pill swapping, like sugar and eggs." One doctor asked a student if she had considered the fact that she "might someday want to marry a man who holds virginity in high regard." Her reply shocked the doctor: "Yes, but I'm not at all sure I want to marry a man like that."[36]

In spite of all the controversy and commotion, by 1967 only 45 percent of the nation's college health services prescribed the pill for students.[37] At KU, the university provided prescriptions only for married women over eighteen and refused them to single women of any age. In 1966, a forum about the policy in the student newspaper generated a flood of letters, all written by male students. Most of the letters focused on student responsibility and called for access to the pill. "Who should make the moral decision, the university or the students themselves?" wrote one of them. But none of these men asked if *women* students should be the ones to make the decision. Finally, in 1967, a letter appeared from a female student: "I take the Pill because I'd rather express my love than repress it. I'm not promiscuous, but once in awhile I meet a 'special' guy. I've seen too many girls on campus totally disregard school for several weeks as they suffer anxiety over a missed menstrual period. . . . If a girl takes one chance a year, that's enough to warrant taking the pill." More noteworthy than this student's comment was the fact that her letter was unsigned. Although all the men signed their letters, as required by the paper's policy, the editors published the woman's letter anonymously. They all agreed that to reveal the name of the one female student who wrote about her sexual experiences and attitudes would damage her reputation.[38]

The sexual revolution did not become meaningful for women until the feminist movement pushed open doors of opportunity that made self-determination possible. Officials who made the pill available to single women in Lawrence, Kansas, had no interest in promoting sexual freedom or women's liberation. Rather, they were motivated by concerns about the population crisis and the need to prevent unwed pregnancy.[39] It wasn't until the late 1960s and early 1970s, when the women's movement gained momentum, that women began to claim the right to sexual and reproductive self-determination. Until then, the pill was just one more contraceptive—not a tool for revolution or emancipation.

EVEN POPULAR CULTURE REFLECTED THE PILL'S LIMITED impact. Hollywood pumped out dozens of movies that explored the sexual revolution and the counterculture of the 1960s, but the pill was absent from the screen until 1967. Curiously, only five films specifically included reference to the pill; four were American and one was British. All four of the American films portray the pill as causing problems rather than resolving them. The pill does not provide the characters with the means to achieve sexual liberation. The film version of Philip Roth's *Goodbye Columbus* is a case in point. The drama surrounding the diaphragm remained in the movie version, but by the time the film came out in 1969, the pill was available, and in new dialogue, Brenda firmly rejects it. In the film, Neil assumes that Brenda is on the pill. As they shower together after a night of lovemaking, Neil casually asks Brenda if she takes the pill every morning. When she responds that she doesn't take the pill, he is shocked. Furious, he warns that she could get pregnant. She replies that the pills make her sick and she doesn't like the side effects. They quarrel but she insists she will not take the pill. Finally she agrees to get a diaphragm.

Other films contained similarly negative messages about the pill. In *The Girl, the Body, and the Pill* (1967) a young woman steals her mother's pills and replaces them with saccharine. The melodrama unfolds when the mother gets pregnant and almost dies from an abortion, prompting the dishonest daughter to rush to her side and beg her forgiveness. *Pickup on 101* (1972) features a free-spirited college student who starts taking the pill. She breaks up with her boyfriend, quits school, and joins a commune. In the end she sees the folly of her ways. *Cactus in the Snow* (1972) follows an eighteen-year-old soldier about to leave for Vietnam and eager to lose his virginity before he goes off to war. The young woman who offers to have sex with him goes into the bathroom to take a birth control pill (erroneously suggesting that the pill can be taken effectively just before intercourse). In the end, the two young virgins decide not to have sex after all, and the young man goes off to Vietnam, where he dies. These were hardly films about sexual liberation.

The one film that featured the pill in a lighthearted way was a British farce, *Prudence and the Pill* (1968). Set among the British upper crust, the film stars Deborah Kerr and David Niven as an unhappily married couple living in separate bedrooms. They have not slept together in years, and each is having an affair and looking for a way out of the marriage. At the same time, their unmarried niece is sleeping with her boyfriend and stealing pills from her mother, replacing them with aspirin.

The idea spreads and soon everyone is replacing aspirin for pills, including the house servant and her lover. In a set of bizarre plot twists, the pill actually serves to reaffirm family values. The films ends with the main characters happily divorced and married to their respective lovers. The camera lingers on the cherubic offspring of the now married couples, whose capers with the pill lead not to sexual revolution but to babies and domestic bliss.[40]

As these films suggest, the pill's liberating potential was not actualized by the sexual revolution. Only when women themselves took control of the pill, not only by consuming it but also by making demands on their sexual partners, doctors, pharmaceutical companies, and lawmakers, would the pill begin to fulfill its potential to change women's lives for the better. Meanwhile, many women believed that there would be no real sexual revolution, and no true equality, until men shared fully in the responsibility for contraception. For that to happen, there would need to be a pill for men.

5

A Pill for Men?

*Seeing over the years how many different forms of
'the Pill' are put onto the market every year, it does
make me wonder why the hell there's no pill for
men yet! . . . Can it really be that hard to come up
with a pill that can make men shoot blanks?*

Leslie C,
age 27, 2008[1]

Of the many hopes that greeted the possibility of hormonal contraceptives, none was more elusive than the
promise of a pill for men. While the arrival of the oral contraceptive for women made headlines around the world, scientists were quietly working on a similar pill for men. But the
male pill never made it to market. In fact, since World War
II, thirteen new contraceptives for women became available—
including various oral contraceptive compounds, IUDs, injectables, and patches—but not one new male method. By the
mid-1990s, only a fraction of the funding for contraceptive

research was dedicated to male methods.[2] Yet, for more than half a century, researchers proclaimed that a pill for men was just around the corner.

In 1969, *Good Housekeeping* enthused, "The notion of a birth control pill for men strikes some people as a kind of science-fiction idea. Actually, development of a male pill is easily possible in the near future—probably within the decade, according to some experts." Describing the many research projects under way to develop a new contraceptive for men, the article concluded that "remarkable progress is being made."[3] In 1976, three scientists predicted that with adequate support, a male pill would be on the market in fifteen years. When that did not happen, the prediction was postponed another twenty years. But the optimism that a male pill would become available "soon" never disappeared and, in fact, still prevails.[4]

Although researchers often questioned whether men would be receptive to a contraceptive pill, surveys indicated that men were willing to share the responsibility for birth control.[5] In 1973, 70 percent of men surveyed in three states and the District of Columbia said they would use a male contraceptive other than condoms or withdrawal. The methods favored by most of the respondents was a pill or injection; 19 percent favored a reversible vasectomy; 84 percent believed that both partners have a responsibility for birth control; and 77 percent said they would help, "financially and morally," in the event of a pregnancy if contraceptives used by either partner failed.[6] But as a practical matter, a male contraceptive would need to have *acceptable* side effects—and most of the methods being developed did not.

From the outset, the problem of side effects plagued the development of a pill for men. As was the case with the female pill, research on a male hormonal contraceptive began in the 1950s and grew out of efforts to treat infertility. Gregory Pincus, while working on the female pill, conducted a small-scale study testing the effects of Enovid on eight male patients in a mental hospital. This ethically reprehensible research, though standard at the time, demonstrated that Enovid had a "sterilizing effect" on men, suggesting that it might provide the basis for a male contraceptive. But the subject pool, besides being very small, was made up of psychotic men, which made it difficult to collect semen. They all suffered serious side effects, such as shrunken testicles. A similar clinical trial took place in 1958 among twenty "healthy adult males" who were prisoners at Oregon State Penitentiary. The study tested two testosterone preparations and one progesterone compound (Enovid). The compounds reduced sperm production to zero. But all the subjects lost sexual desire and had difficulty getting erections and producing seminal fluid.

In 1963 another study tested a male contraceptive on thirty-nine inmates at the same prison. The compound halted sperm production without affecting libido. But when a man who took the pill was released from prison and went out drinking, he became violently ill and had to be hospitalized. Although it was possible for men taking the pill to refrain from alcohol in order to avoid serious health risks, the potentially dangerous combination of alcohol and hormones put an end to this birth control alternative.

Additional small-scale tests continued through the 1970s in the United States and Europe. Male prisoners were commonly used in these trials—a standard practice that continued well into the 1980s. All of these studies showed promising results, but problematic side effects remained.[7] Moreover, the advantages of using institutionalized men who could be frequently monitored were diminished by the fact that these subjects were not having sex with women. The controlled experiments, therefore, did not demonstrate how a particular compound might work in a typical heterosexual relationship.

The problem of overpopulation motivated and legitimized research for a male pill, as it had for the female pill. As one scientist warned, "Because of the immensity and seriousness of human population growth every avenue should continue to be explored and we should be unwise to neglect the male approach."[8] In the developing world, especially in overcrowded China and India, governments pushed for an effective male contraceptive. In the 1960s, Premier Chou En-Lai of China and India's Prime Minister Indira Gandhi called for new technologies. In 1961, Gandhi tried to pass a law for large-scale forced sterilization on men. The proposal generated such protest it resulted in the fall of her cabinet. Gandhi then turned to promoting new methods of birth control: "Family planning programs are awaiting a big breakthrough; without a safe, preferably oral drug which women and men can take, no amount of government commitment and political determination will avail."[9]

China did not wait for such a breakthrough. Starting in 1972, China began clinical trials of Gossypol, a male contraceptive, on 14,000 men. China was able to recruit these men because of the one-child law, which made contraception mandatory. News of the study finally reached the West in 1979 when a group of

American researchers visited China. Gossypol seemed promising until toxic side effects began to appear, including diarrhea, circulatory problems, heart failure, and permanent sterility.[10]

Funding for the Gossypol study and other research on male contraceptives came from the World Health Organization (WHO). A 1978 article in the WHO bulletin explained, "In the past, emphasis has been placed on the development and use of contraceptive methods for women but, with increasing publicity on the problems associated with the use of oral estrogen-gestagen contraceptives, the role of the male in contraceptive practice is re-examined . . . and research into new methods is being stimulated." On the need for this shift in emphasis, WHO officials and Western feminists agreed.[11]

While Asian leaders called for a male pill to control population, feminists called for the development of a male contraceptive so that men could share the risks and responsibilities of birth control. Barbara Seaman, author of *The Doctors' Case Against the Pill*, insisted that the problem was sexism: "If you doubt that there has been sex discrimination in the development of the pill, try to answer this question: Why isn't there a pill for men?. . . . It is because women have always had to bear most of the risks associated with sex and reproduction."[12]

Not all feminists agreed that women should relinquish contraceptive responsibility to men. In fact, from the very beginning of their efforts to develop the birth control pill, Margaret Sanger and Katharine McCormick were adamant that contraception be entirely in the hands of women. McCormick said she "didn't give a hoot for a male contraceptive."[13] The two pioneers strongly believed that women should decide when and if they wanted to have babies, and that they should have a safe and effective means to prevent pregnancy. They pushed for the pill because it would give women that control.

Within a few years of the pill's FDA approval, however, risks and side effects emerged that Sanger and McCormick had not anticipated. By the mid-1960s, angry women were writing to John Rock and Gregory Pincus demanding a pill for men. "Why don't you men take the contraceptive pills?" wrote one irate woman. "Stop making us—the women—guinea pigs in this experiment. . . . Why don't men mature and understand that there are desires in life besides excessive use of your love-stick?" Another wrote, "Why is it that the billions of words being written, printed, [and] spoken now on the subject of the Population Explosion [are] directed to WOMEN? All about what Women can and should DO, but NOT ONE WORD have I read or heard directed towards MEN." One letter writer suggested clamps for men "such as cattlemen use on bulls." A mother of three and grandmother of nine wrote in 1963, "The women more than do their share. The men are the most passionate, so why not control them for a change? . . . Please let us women have a rest from pills and put the cure where it belongs—on men." Rock responded with the optimism characteristic of the researchers at the time: "It will not be long now when you can feel that you are getting even."[14]

Rock was wrong. The male pill was nowhere in sight. Researchers felt stymied by what seemed to be insurmountable hurdles standing in the way. The most intractable were the men themselves. In 1970, *Boston Globe* columnist Dr. Lindsay R. Curtis relayed a conversation he had with a woman he identified as Helen, an ardent feminist who was "disgusted" with the lack of progress on a male pill. "It's the same old story, male domination. . . . Why not let the ever-loving husband take his turn and allow a few experiments performed on him for a change?" Dr. Curtis responded by explaining that there were male contraceptives in the works, but that more time was needed to test their safety and effectiveness. He also noted that men do not have the same stake in contraception: "What it boils down to is this: Women can get pregnant; men can't." There were also psychological effects. "Generally speaking, a man equates his ability to impregnate a woman with masculinity. And all too often the loss of such ability really deflates his ego." Helen replied, "Might be just what a lot of egotistical males need."[15] Needed or not, the male libido seemed to be the primary preoccupation in any discussion of a pill for men. Although there was evidence that the oral contraceptive could negatively affect women's sex drive, that particular side effect was dismissed as unimportant.

As early as 1965, Gregory Pincus articulated the problem: "Male volunteers for fertility control studies may be numbered in the low hundreds, whereas women have volunteered for similar studies by the thousands. . . . He [the human male] has psychological aversions to experimenting with sexual functions. . . . Perhaps experimental studies of fertility control in men should be preceded by a thorough investigation of male attitudes."[16] In the 1970s, sexuality remained a central concern in the male contraceptive trials. A 1974 report to the World Health Organization urged researchers to develop a reversible male contraceptive that would not compromise libido or potency. Even though male sexual functioning improved in clinical trials as researchers experimented with new compounds, worries about reduced libido continued to discourage men from volunteering for studies. One researcher believed that extensive education would be necessary because the "delicate male psyche equates virility with fertility."[17] As late as the 1990s, a Dutch researcher noted, "The Pill for men inhibits libido. This might be considered an advantage—refraining from sex constitutes a perfect contraceptive—but men don't take the Pill to refrain from sex."[18]

IN SPITE OF MEN'S RELUCTANCE TO TAMPER WITH their sexual functions, news of problems associated with the oral contraceptives for women put new pressures on them. Senate hearings in 1970 on the safety of the pill prompted 18 percent of women taking oral contraceptives to discontinue use, leading to a renewed interest in male options. But men themselves were not clamoring for a pill. They remained conspicuously silent on the matter. Many did step up to the plate to take responsibility for contraception, but they turned to tried-and-true methods: the condom and vasectomy. According to a 1970 headline in the *Washington Post*: "Pill scare, lib movement place birth onus on male." The article pointed out that condoms, after declining in sales in the mid-1960s, were selling better than ever following the Senate hearings. Now women as well as men were buying them. Ads for condoms also began to appear in the popular press, with catchy messages such as "90 percent of all people are caused by accidents."[19]

At the same time, articles in the popular press began to promote vasectomies. In 1971, *Look* magazine's column "For Men

Only" touted "Foolproof Birth Control" and claimed that a "simple 15-minute operation is putting the pleasure back in marital relations."[20] Although the procedure was growing in popularity, many men were still uneasy about going under the knife. One nervous man wrote to a doctor at the *Boston Globe* asking about the effectiveness, reversibility, and side effects of the operation: "And most important, is there any decrease in a man's sex drive or potency?" The doctor reassured the man that his libido would not be affected.[21]

Not all the press coverage was so reassuring. The cover story of *Esquire* in June 1972 carried the headline "All about Vasectomies (scared?)." Evoking men's anxieties about both feminism and vasectomies, the photo on the cover pictured a woman surgeon in scrubs, gloves, and mask, with surgical scissors in one hand and scalpel in the other. The long article, titled "The Incision Decision," covers "a burgeoning brotherhood of men who had taken the ultimate step in contraception: . . . vasectomy." While most media coverage of vasectomies emphasized the relative safety and effectiveness of the procedure, *Esquire* detailed all the dangers and side effects, along with physical, psychological, and psychosexual difficulties. Chastising leaders for their failure to develop safe and effective alternatives to the frightening procedure, the author concluded that "vasectomy is a direct indictment of our refusal . . . to develop, test and distribute an entire spectrum of contraceptive drugs and devices that would allow individual men and women to choose one they can use without playing roulette with their health."[22]

In spite of calls for new methods, research on male contraception continued at a snail's pace. Whether or not men would actually take a contraceptive pill if one were developed, the scientific community assumed they would not. Contraceptive development was falling victim to the increasing skepticism and scrutiny directed at the pharmaceutical industry and the medical profession. In 1970 an article in *Today's Health* noted that the "Pill Panic" caused by recent revelations of the dangers of oral contraceptives would inhibit research efforts to find a male method, just at the time when women were clamoring for men to share the risks. The pill had simultaneously raised the bar for effective and convenient birth control and aroused fears of health consequences.[23]

More significant than the research hurdles to developing male contraceptives was the widespread and continuing belief that women would accept the risks, discomforts, and physical intrusions required to sabotage their fertility, but men would not. These ideas were so deeply held that reversals of this arrangement seemed absurd. Two widely circulated parodies of contraceptive guidelines make the point. In 1971, a spoof in the *Village Voice* offered a fictional guide to men to help them choose an appropriate form of birth control. To select among the "fine methods available to the modern husband," the author advised, "Consult a qualified urologist. She will explain to you several methods. . . . One widely used method is the insertion of sperm-killing liquid into the urethra before intercourse. She (your doctor) will show you how. . . . The other widely used method is of course the Capsule. . . . There are minor undesirable side-effects in some men: you may gain weight around the abdomen or buttocks, get white pigmentless patches on your face (which you may be able to conceal with a beard or face-bronzer), or suffer some morning nausea. But be patient—these effects often decrease or even disappear after a few months. The one serious drawback of the Capsule is that you are several times more likely than otherwise to suffer eventually from prostate cancer or fatal blood clots. But these ailments are relatively uncommon anyway, so that many couples consider it worth the risk, especially since this is the one method that is 100 percent effective."[24]

In 1980, after the Dalkon Shield disaster, in which eighteen women died and hundreds of thousands others suffered serious infections of the uterus requiring hysterectomies as the result of the faulty design of the widely used intrauterine device (IUD), another satire circulated in the alternative press. With a graphic illustration covering half the page, *Spare Rib* announced a new male contraceptive, the IPD (intrapenile device), to be marketed under the trade name "Umbrelly." At the "American Women's Surgical Symposium in Ann Arbor, Michigan," a "Dr. Sophie Merkin" announced the results of a study of the Umbrelly conducted on 763 male students at a large Midwestern university. The IPD "resembles a tiny folded umbrella which is inserted through the head of the penis and pushed into the scrotum with a plungerlike instrument. Occasionally there is perforation of the scrotum but this is disregarded since it is known that the male has few nerve endings in this area of his body. The underside of the umbrella contains a spermicidal jelly, hence the name 'Umbrelly.'" Dr. Merkin reported that of the students tested with the device, "only two died of scrotal infection, only 20 experienced swelling of the tissues. Three developed cancer of the testicles, and 13 were too depressed to have an erection." She also noted cramping, bleeding, and abdominal pain, but insisted that these symptoms were probably temporary and would likely disappear within a year. Although there were a few cases of "massive scrotal infection necessitating the surgical removal of the testicles," this complication was too rare to be statistically important. "She and other distinguished members of the Women's College of Surgeons agreed that the benefits far outweighed the risk to any individual man."[25]

The biting satire gave voice to the concerns of many women that if men faced the same sorts of discomforts, dangers, and complications that women risked from recently developed contraceptives, such products would never reach the market. This spoof effectively made the point that men would never approve, much less consume, products that would cause them such pain and danger.

Although an intrapenile device remained in the realm of fantasy, researchers worked on a number of male contraceptive compounds and devices. In 1972, *Life* ran a story on "Male Contraception with a Twist." Illustrating the article was a magnified image of two tiny, T-shaped, gold and stainless steel "sperm switches." "The long tubes of these microvalves . . . fit snugly inside a sperm duct. In a simple procedure, a doctor merely adjusts the stem to turn sperm flow on or off." The good news for men was that "these new sperm switches will let a man have his fertility turned on and off at will. They do not interfere with normal sexual function." Louis Bucalo, a microcomponent engineer, designed the devices, which were tested at New York Medical College on thirty volunteers. At the time, it appeared that the device was safe and effective. "Conceivably . . . a man might have the devices implanted when he is young, and then have them turned on only once or twice in his lifetime when he wants to produce children." The author predicted that if the testing continued to go well, "the sperm switches will be available within 18 months." The device was expected to be expensive, "but so is an unwanted pregnancy and so, over the years, is a regimen of birth control pills." *Life* also noted that vasectomies were becoming increasingly popular, encouraged in part by the establishment of sperm banks across the country and observed that "over 400 normal children have been produced by artificial insemination using frozen sperm."[26] The "sperm switches," however, never reached the market. Although research continued, the risk of scar tissue causing permanent sterility was never successfully resolved.

Another group of researchers tried to develop a reversible vasectomy by using a temporary implant inserted into the vas that could be removed. In theory, the process could be reversed several times as the man wishes to be fertile or infertile. But the researchers were unable to say when such an operation might be available for use on a human male.[27] By 1983, other promising designs were in the works. One was a contraceptive cream that combined testosterone with estrogen that men would rub onto their abdomen and chest. The compound would inhibit sperm production without affecting male sex drive and potency. But some scientists were cautious about its efficiency because the cream had not been shown to turn off sperm production completely. Although it seemed to hold some promise, the contraceptive ointment never made it to clinical trials.[28]

Even the lowly jockstrap seemed to offer contraceptive potential. In 1975, *Esquire*, hostile to the idea of vasectomies, waxed enthusiastic about this benign undergarment: "The jockstrap, its place in sports history already snugly secure . . . will be credited with contributing mightily to the protection of mankind from grievous pain, injury, insult *and*, it now appears tantalizingly possible, *overpopulation*." The article quoted John Rock, who noted that sperm output declines when the testicles are heated. "Daily wear of a well-fitting, closely knit jockstrap results in infertility after four weeks." Although the jockstrap was hardly foolproof, *Esquire* found it to be much preferable to other methods that might emasculate the man. According to Dr. Sheldon Segal of the Population Council, "A man *could* take his wife's oral contraceptives and he'd be incapable of fertilizing her within fourteen days, but his libido would be shot to hell, too," and another researcher warned, "Start interfering with sperm production and before you know it you've got a pussycat."[29]

Theoretically, however, the jockstrap idea had potential. According to Dr. Mostafa S. Fahim, a reproductive pharmacologist, "If we're ever going to have any impact on world overpopulation, we've got to have a contraceptive that is neither surgical nor pharmacological, something even the poorest and most illiterate can make use of." Using the concept of heat to develop new male methods, he constructed a device to warm the testicles to the level that would inhibit sperm production. It was a "water-activated battery" that could heat up to 230 degrees Fahrenheit. "Inserted in a spongelike material, it can easily be shaped into a pouch suitable for heating the testes." The pouch was to be worn half an hour at a time and then discarded. Fahim pointed out that the device was preferable to a vasectomy because it was nonsurgical and reversible. "Things look very good now, but we must still perform complex, long-term genetic and biochemical tests on a large number of subjects. We mustn't be hasty. We don't want this to be like The Pill and now, perhaps, vasectomy, where troubles begin to manifest themselves years after millions of people have already become involved."[30] This device, like the others, never made it to market.

While these various alternatives were being studied, researchers continued their efforts to develop a contraceptive pill, injection, or vaccine for men. In the late 1960s, one drug under consideration was Agent U5897, a "common industrial compound used in the manufacture of dynamite" that promised to be free of the serious drawbacks that had hampered the development of the male pill, especially the problem of reduced libido. U5897 was not ready for human trials, however, because of toxic side effects. The silver lining in the research was the discovery that the drug was effective in stemming the fertility of laboratory rats, suggesting that even if the drug was not practical for humans, it could be used to reduce the population of rodents. The *Minneapolis Tribune* reported this finding under the unfortunate headline, "Antifertility Drug Developed for Men, Rats."[31]

With all the hormonal methods being tested, scientists actually discovered an effective vaccine that completely stopped the production of sperm without interfering with sex drive. But it had an unacceptable side effect. According to the researchers studying the vaccine, "There is one drawback which indirectly affects libido, and because of this drawback, I quite honestly doubt we'll ever be able to use the vaccine. The testes get smaller—about a third smaller—so this approach will never work. The psychological trauma of shrinking testes just cannot be overcome."[32] Antifertility injections were also under scrutiny as early as the 1960s, but they had the same problem. *Good Housekeeping* reported that investigators were searching for methods that would not reduce the size of the testicles. Other promising possibilities included a capsule containing a synthetic male hormone that would be implanted under the skin to prevent sperm formation. Removing the capsule would restore fertility (much like Norplant for women).[33]

In 1981, researchers at Vanderbilt University reported tests of a daily injection for men of the drug luteinizing hormone–releasing hormone, or LHRH, that suppressed sperm production and lowered testosterone. When it was tested on eight men between the ages of twenty-eight and forty-two, the injections were found to be nontoxic, and all subjects regained their fertility after discontinuing use. But yet again, some of the volunteers experienced a loss of sex drive, impotence, and "momentary increases in body temperature, or so-called hot flashes, such as those experienced by women after menopause." The scientists began working on a compound that would eliminate the side effects and said that it could take several years before the drug would be considered safe for marketing.[34]

Six years later, the *New York Times* reported that researchers were testing another birth control injection for men, which used a synthetic form of testosterone to inhibit the production of sperm. Under the auspices of the World Health Organization, the medication was being tested in several countries, including the United States, where thirty Seattle men were involved in the trials. Though the results didn't show any negative effects on sex drive or other "personality factors," the injections were not 100 percent effective. Researchers were trying to refine the dosage to lower the failure rate to less than 1 percent. The major hurdle was that the contraceptive required a weekly injection. Of course, those scientists did not seem to consider it impractical for women to consume a pill every day. But they believed that men would be unwilling to take an injection every week.[35]

SCIENTISTS WHO DEVOTED YEARS OF WORK TRYING to develop an effective and acceptable male contraceptive bristled at the accusation that chauvinism prevented the introduction of a contraceptive for men. Writing in 1972, Dr. Sheldon Segal explained that it is much more difficult to intervene in the physiological and chemical constitution of the male reproductive system.[36] A quarter of a century later, researchers made a similar point: "All you have to do with women is to knock out the production of one egg per month, but men produce something like 250 million sperm cells per ejaculation. Suppressing this gigantic factory of sperm production in men is a lot more difficult."[37]

Other scientists dissented from this view, arguing that it was not necessarily more complicated to prevent sperm production than to inhibit ovulation. Nevertheless, most agreed that for a variety of reasons, ranging from human biology to funding and testing constraints, the development of a male pill would be difficult. In 1983, in her column in the *New York Times*, Jane Brody supported the claim that physiology was the greatest barrier to male contraception. Noting that many feminists believed that "male researchers feel more comfortable tampering with a woman's physiology than with their own," she nonetheless agreed with the view that "basic biology remains the greatest barrier to developing male contraceptives." Taking on the single most controversial point in any discussion of a male pill, she continued, "The organ that produces sperm also makes the male sex hormone testosterone, which is responsible for libido, potency and secondary sex characteristics. . . . By contrast, ovarian function need not be wholly suppressed to prevent ovulation. And since a woman's libido is not a function of ovarian hormones, but of other sex hormones produced in the adrenal glands, side effects are more easily avoided."[38]

A month later, the *New York Times* editorialized that while men and women should share the responsibility for birth control, it would probably be twenty years before a new male contraceptive would be available. The editorial promoted vasectomies and cited a study showing the procedure to be safe and effective. Yet it concluded that the ideal birth control was still a long way off: "Someday somebody somewhere will develop the perfect contraceptive, suitable for both sexes with no health risk whatever."[39]

There were, of course, cultural reasons for the relative lack of attention to male contraception. The emphasis on women is embedded in the institutional frameworks of science, medicine, and pharmaceuticals. Both women and men think of reproduction in terms of women's bodies and of birth control as a woman's responsibility. The fact that the medical profession generally considers reproduction a female concern has led to a scarcity of doctors trained in male reproductive medicine and a shortage of scientists interested in working on male contraception. Ronald Ericsson, one of the researchers in the field of male contraception, complained in 1973 that male contraceptive research "is almost an illegitimate specialty within reproductive biology." As late as the 1990s, male contraceptive researchers complained that they were considered "second-class scientists."[40]

Some researchers speculated that the heightened scrutiny of new pharmaceuticals made it more difficult and time-consuming to gain approval for human trials and bring new methods to market. As early as 1977, Dr. Don Fawcett of the Harvard Medical School warned that it would be many years before "*she* will ask *him*, 'Did you take your pill today, dear?' " He noted that since the FDA approved the pill in 1960, much stricter regulations governing experimentation on human subjects had been put into place, hampering the search for a male pill. "When [the FDA] didn't approve thalidomide [the drug that caused thousands of severe birth defects in Europe] for marketing, that put them on the map, and so now the tendency is to be extra cautious. If the FDA official has even the slightest doubt, the easiest thing for him (sic) to do is to say, 'go back and do 1000 more rats.' " (The FDA official who blocked approval of thalidomide was, in fact, a *she*—Frances Oldham Kelsey.)[41] Regulations aside, there was still the problem of the men themselves. "There is nothing inherently difficult about finding chemicals to inhibit male reproductive capacities," Fawcett explained, but the question remained, "Will they use it? Will men, even in a pill-popping society like ours, take to taking the pill?" He predicted that older men might resist but that young men would be open to the idea.[42]

Indeed, he may have been right. A generation after Fawcett's prediction, men's reluctance may be declining. In the wake of the feminist challenge to traditional gender norms, a new concept of manhood that includes qualities of caring and taking responsibility has eroded earlier attitudes that equated masculinity with sexual conquest. Although none claimed that male contraceptives would contribute to men's freedom or reproductive rights, men who participated in clinical trials of new contraceptives saw themselves as caring partners. In 2008, twenty-three-year-old Erin M wrote in response to an online survey that it was "unfortunate that male hormonal contraceptives are not on the market, because my husband would volunteer for it (we've talked about it)." She worried, however, about its safety: "I would be uncomfortable with that until male birth control had been well tested, though."[43]

To persuade volunteers to participate in studies, researchers appealed to their sense of masculine bravery and heroism. Making this point explicit was a poster used to recruit volunteers in Edinburgh, Scotland. Next to an image of an astronaut perched on the surface of the moon were bold letters proclaiming, "FIRST MAN ON THE PILL." By the early twenty-first century, as researchers continued to work on developing a male contraceptive pill, most believed that men would be receptive, especially those in stable relationships. Noted one doctor: "It won't work for the 17-year-old at the nightclub looking for a contraceptive but will for men in relationships." Another noted that the question of trust would be all important: "A woman would be mad to believe a chap she met in a night club who said: you're all right love, I'm on the Pill."[44]

By 2008, that scenario seemed not so absurd. Kansas City journalist Jonathan Bender wrote that with new male contraceptives due within a year, "The hotel bar pick up will have a delightfully different spin. So next year when a guy says, 'Don't worry, I'm on the pill,' you can relax." Bender welcomed the introduction of a male pill, injection, or patch. Noting that the major side effects appeared to be weight gain and increased muscle mass, he quipped, "But hey who doesn't like bigger pecs?"[45] (The comment echoed the happy responses of some female pill users who discovered that the pill enlarged their breasts.)

NO LONGER A SPOOF OF ABSURDLY REVERSED GENDER roles, in the twenty-first century many of the leading physicians and scientists involved in developing male contraceptives are women. Dr. Andrea Coviello, one of the researchers involved in testing a microcapsule injected under the skin that releases testosterone over three months, noted that the technology has been developed but cautioned that the availability of the new method depended on continued funding. Using methods similar to the oral contraceptive for women, the male compound would use hormones such as testosterone and progestins to turn off sperm production. According to Dr. Christina Wang, who is directing the study at Harbor-UCLA Medical Center in Los Angeles, the first male hormonal contraceptive would probably be an injectable or an implant similar to Norplant for women. Studies under way suggest that the implants are "safe, effective, inexpensive, and entirely reversible." She predicted FDA approval within five years. The California researchers are collaborating with scientists in China, where

1,000 men are involved in clinical trials to develop low-cost, effective, and reversible male contraceptives with minimal side effects. Dr. Wang notes that there is greater interest in male contraception, and more funding available worldwide, than ever before.[46]

Within the United States, men involved in the studies reported positive results. Larry Setlow, a thirty-nine-year-old computer programmer in Seattle, volunteered for three different clinical trials of pills and injections. "I never had any real noticeable side effects. I didn't notice any mood changes. I may have put on a little weight. . . . They all worked really well and I was able to look at my lab results and see my sperm count drop to zero." Forty-five-year-old Quentin Brown, a married father of three who lives in Los Angeles, reported no significant problems after taking hormonal contraceptives for more than a year. His motivation for helping to develop the pill was hardly in support of feminism, however. "It is time for men to have some control. I think it would empower men and deter some women out there from their nefarious plans. Some women are out there to use men to get pregnant. This could deter women from doing this. An athlete or a singer is someone who could be a target and they could put a stop to that."[47]

Men were not the only ones to raise the issue of trust. Twenty-eight-year-old Mary B saw the other side of it: "I have heard women say that they'd be against a male pill because they wouldn't trust men to take it. Of course that's silly. The point of a male pill isn't that it allows you to stop taking it. It's just that you have twice the protection. Also, I think that it will force men to be more responsible towards children they did father. No longer would the 'she tricked me' option be on the table."[48]

While some men perceived potential benefits, others remained reluctant. Forty-year-old Stuart H, a single college administrator, said he would welcome a method for men but not one that involved taking hormones: "I would rather rely on a solution that doesn't involve medicating myself, and the problems women have had with hormone therapy doesn't make me anxious to want to sign on to taking a hormone-type therapy."[49] Many women, however, see it as a matter of fairness and equality. Kelly H was "amused and pissed off" to hear that "men refused to consider a male contraceptive until there was some non-chemical breakthrough because they were afraid of what the chemicals and hormones might do to their bodies and 'masculinity.' I told my mother that they obviously weren't worried about the damage to *women*'s bodies over multiple years of ingesting 'dangerous' chemicals and hormones. Sexist fuckers."[50]

In keeping with the values of her Southern Baptist upbringing in rural Oklahoma, twenty-eight-year-old Cathy S and her husband of seven years married as virgins. But her traditional ideals did not stand in the way of her belief in equality for women. "I like the idea of a male birth control pill—something that would give men the freedom and responsibility of reproductive choice. It would be one more step toward egalitarianism."[51] Rachel A, age twenty-eight, resents "that birth control is now my sole responsibility. I'd feel better about it if [my boyfriend] had to pop a pill everyday at the same time too." At age seventeen, Donna H was already annoyed and frustrated: "I have to take a pill and use hormones to control fertility but men do not." Susan G, a twenty-two-year-old student, lamented, "What kind of a culture thinks it's okay to mess with a woman's chemistry and fecundity, but to even consider a pill that does the same for men is completely ludicrous?"[52]

In 2008, MSNBC repeated a decades-old claim: "For the first time, a safe, effective and reversible hormonal male contraceptive appears to be within reach."[53] Studies remain under way all across the globe. The World Health Organization, which has long supported research on male contraceptives, reports a great deal of success with compounds under study and no difficulty finding recruits to volunteer for the clinical trials. Optimistic scientists proclaim that a new male contraceptive is just around the corner, as they have predicted for half a century. But the same question remains: Will men take it?

No such question stood in the way of another pharmaceutical product aimed at men's sex organs: Viagra. In the midst of continuing efforts to secure funding for the development of a hormonal contraceptive that men would take, the pharmaceutical industry poured massive resources into developing a pill for men that would do just the opposite. Viagra hit the U.S. market in 1998 and quickly became the most successful prescription drug ever launched in the United States, despite the fact that it carries serious health risks.[54] Apparently, a pill that enhances the potential for men to impregnate women is considerably more marketable than one that diminishes that possibility.

6

Questioning Authority

I am often asked if I had a bad experience with the pill. I never took it, nor did my daughters, but, like other women of my generation, I learned early that: gynecologists tend to interfere too much with natural processes, and, they adopt new technologies without adequate evaluation.

Barbara Seaman,
The Doctors' Case Against the Pill[1]

When the pill arrived in 1960, it rode the crest of the wave of optimism, faith in scientific progress, and a belief that professional experts could guide the world to a better future. The pill promised to fulfill the hopes of the new era. As the decade unfolded, however, dissent, distrust, and rebellion emerged to challenge the certainties that seemed to prevail in the early 1960s. After the pill's celebrated debut and its embrace by millions of women, it also became the focus of widespread challenges to the authority of religious leaders, doctors, pharmaceutical companies, and lawmakers. Women led the charge against the mostly male experts and officials who prohibited or limited access to the pill, controlled information about it, and dismissed women's concerns about risks and side effects.

Initially, many American women defied religious or governmental authority simply by taking the pill. The Catholic Church banned the use of contraceptives, yet many Catholics took the pill anyway. Women also undermined the law. In 1960, thirty states still had laws restricting the advertising and sale of contraceptives. Massachusetts and Connecticut banned contraception outright. In Connecticut, contraceptive use was punishable by a $50 fine or imprisonment for up to one year.[2] Yet the laws did not prevent women who wanted the pill from getting it. Frustrated by laws that turned women as well as their doctors into criminals, in 1961 Estelle Griswold, executive director of the Planned Parenthood League of Connecticut, and Dr. C. Lee Buxton, chair of the Department of Obstetrics at Yale University School of Medicine, opened a birth control clinic with the intent to challenge the law's constitutionality. Their act of civil disobedience succeeded in getting them arrested and prosecuted, and their case went all the way to the Supreme Court. In 1965, in *Griswold v. Connecticut*, the Supreme Court invalidated the Connecticut law on the grounds that the constitutional right to privacy guaranteed married couples the right to make their own decisions about birth control. In 1972, in *Eisenstadt v. Baird*, the Supreme Court extended that right to unmarried individuals.[3]

The pill was a factor in the increasing autonomy of women to assert their independence and make demands on professional experts and religious authorities—or to reject their advice altogether. The Civil Rights movement, the antiwar movement, the feminist movement, and the sexual revolution—all of this activism against failed national policies, gender discrimination, racial oppression, and rigid sexual codes—provided the context in which women took matters related to the pill into their own hands. By the mid-1960s, it was already becoming obvious that the pill was not a panacea for the world's problems. But it was clearly a boon for individual women. Oral contraceptives continued to be enormously popular, widely prescribed, and highly effective. At the same time, as a flash point for so many conflicts and controversies, the pill became a vehicle for new laws, policies, and behaviors that altered the relationship between institutional authorities and individuals.

The most formidable institutional foe of the pill was the Catholic Church. Initially, it looked as though the Church's position might be softening. Within a few months of the FDA's approval, the nation elected its first Catholic president, John F. Kennedy. In a marked contrast to his predecessor, Dwight D. Eisenhower, who had insisted that contraception was not a matter for public policy, the Catholic Kennedy supported family planning. In 1964, a physician from the Alliance for Progress went to Rome to discuss South American population programs with the Pope, where he received a "warm reception." The Church appeared to be on the verge of approving the use of contraceptives. According to *The Nation*, it looked like the "end of a taboo."[4]

Catholics comprised a quarter of the American population, but among this huge group and their clergy there was no prevailing consensus about birth control. As Church leaders debated the moral and theological questions surrounding contraception, Catholic women and men struggled to reconcile their faith with their personal needs and desires.[5] Looking back on his early adulthood, Colin S expressed the dilemma facing millions of American Catholics who grappled with the issue. A self-described "good Catholic boy," he entered college in the late 1950s, attended Mass, and didn't question the Church's position on birth control. But in his junior year his girlfriend became pregnant. "Fortunately, or unfortunately, getting one's girl pregnant was not a unique event on my all-male campus," he recalled. "In my fraternity of sixty men, nine were married during my senior year. So we married in February, but she miscarried immediately." Even though they had already experienced an unplanned pregnancy, he says, "We didn't use birth control, except a lame attempt at the rhythm method, and I continued struggling with the ethics of birth control. Although I was not practicing my faith regularly, we had been married in the church, and I vaguely felt that birth control was wrong, but I wanted to take a critical look at the issue."

For a class assignment to speak on a controversial subject, he chose the issue of the Church's position on birth control. "I spoke to the Priest and to other Catholic students, and gave a speech that recited the Catholic position: God created sex for the primary purpose of reproduction; artificial contraception prevents that primary purpose and is therefore against the will of God." Having persuaded himself, he tried to persuade his wife. "She didn't want to get pregnant, but was willing to go along with my conclusion that the rhythm method was the proper approach. It was about as effective as prayer as a contraceptive strategy, however, and in the spring of senior year, she got pregnant." Although they welcomed the baby, born in 1961, by that time the pill was available, and after much soul-searching they decided that "practical economics outweighed the position of the Church." His wife went on the pill.[6]

Like Colin and his wife, thousands of American Catholics were rejecting the Church's ban. Many Catholic leaders and clergy were also calling for change. The popular press was filled with vehement arguments calling on the Vatican to allow for the use of contraceptives. According to *The Christian Century* in 1963, "There can be no doubt that the Roman Catholic Church is taking the wraps off the issue of birth control." Father John A. O'Brien, a Catholic priest and professor of theology at the University of Notre Dame, told *U.S. News & World Report* that there was a large area of agreement among Catholics, Protestants, and Jews on the need for family planning. Although he noted that the only sanctioned method at the time was rhythm, his support for family planning among Catholics pointed the way toward a liberalized policy.[7]

In 1964, Dr. Robert E. Hall, the director of the birth control clinic of Columbia-Presbyterian Medical Center in New York, writing in *The Nation*, called upon the Ecumenical Council, which was reconvening in Rome, to approve family planning. Noting that half of all Catholics admitted to using artificial contraceptives, he railed at the Church's stubborn insistence on condemning birth control. He dismissed the Church's approval of the rhythm method, saying, "Rhythm is not birth control at all, it is *sex control*."[8]

As Catholic doctors and clergy pushed Church authorities to lift the ban, it appeared to many proponents that the pill might foster that change.[9] One of the most influential voices advocating change in the official Catholic position was John Rock, a devout and observant Catholic. A solid Republican for most of his life and no fan of sexual experimentation outside of marriage, Rock, along with many other Catholics, held that contraception was sometimes medically necessary and often personally desirable as a means to maintain happy marriages and well-planned families. Rock believed that married couples should have as many children as they could support but that contraception was important for those who could not afford large families. When the pill became available, he and many others believed that the Church would approve its use.[10]

Long before Rock became involved in the development and testing of the pill, he had promoted the use of contraception. Although he was a Catholic doctor practicing in Massachusetts, where disseminating birth control information or devices was against the law, as early as the 1940s he regularly taught his students at Harvard Medical School how to insert diaphragms. When he began clinical trials of hormonal contraceptives, he thought that the pill offered a means of birth control that the Church could accept. Because the pill simply repressed ovulation and replicated the body's hormonal condition in early pregnancy, Rock argued that the pill didn't obstruct the union of egg and sperm because there would be no egg available to fertilize. Nor did the pill block, harm, or destroy the human seed. In that sense it was unlike all the other barrier or chemical methods that had come before. Rock claimed that the pill was not an "artificial" form of birth control because it worked on the same principle as the rhythm method, which the Church approved, by extending the "safe" period throughout the woman's cycle. It was, in that sense, a "natural" form of contraception and therefore should be acceptable to the Church. In 1963, Rock directly challenged the Church with the publication of his book *The Time Has Come: A Catholic Doctor's Proposals to End the Battle over Birth Control.*[11]

John Rock was hardly a radical, but he held beliefs that directly contradicted long-standing Church teachings. The Church had affirmed its opposition to contraception in 1931 when Pope Pius XI issued *Casti Canubii*, a papal decree that condemned all forms of artificial birth control but allowed for periodic abstinence if there were compelling reasons to avoid pregnancy. In 1950 and 1951 his successor, Pope Pius XII, expanded the exception by approving the rhythm method as an acceptable means of birth control in cases of adverse medical, economic, eugenic, or social circumstances.

Many Catholics expected further loosening of the ban, especially in the wake of Vatican II. Pope John XXIII convened the Second Vatican Council in 1962, a gigantic gathering that is still considered one of the largest meetings in world history. Each fall from 1962 through 1965, 2,400 bishops from all over the world, along with thousands of aides, advisers, and religious leaders, met at the Vatican to debate, discuss, and develop new policies that would alter Church custom around the world. Although Church dogma remained intact, Vatican II brought a number of reforms that modernized Church practices.[12] It also opened the way for clergy as well as lay Catholics to discuss and challenge the dictates coming from Rome. Vatican II led many to believe that the Church's position on contraception might be relaxed. Indeed, Pope John was putting together a committee to consider the matter shortly before his death in 1963. Although he died without making any changes in the Church's birth control ban, his legacy included an empowered laity that began to speak out on the issue, as well as a clergy that was divided on the matter. It fell to Pope Paul VI to resolve things.

Anticipation ran high. Even folk singer and songwriter Pete Seeger expressed the optimism of Catholics in his 1966 ballad, *The Pill*. In the song a woman with a house full of children vows she won't have any more because the Church is going to "bless the pill." She buys a package of pills so she will be ready when they receive the expected message from the Pope. Waiting anxiously, she hopes for the Pope's OK "before my man comes in."[13] But the hopes Seeger's song expressed were dashed.

In 1964, Pope Paul appointed a commission on birth control to advise him on the matter. The following year the commission met in closed session, and the Pope pressed for a clear recommendation. But the deliberations continued for years. In 1967, the commission's report was leaked to the press, revealing that a significant majority of its members had concluded that artificial birth control was acceptable. Those in favor of allowing contraception included sixty out of sixty-four theologians on the commission, and nine of the fifteen cardinals. The minority issued a separate report, calling for a continuation of the Church's ban. After much "anguish," the Pope issued a formal encyclical, *Humanae Vitae* (*Of Human Life*), in 1968, siding with the minority and reaffirming the Church's ban on any form of artificial birth control.[14]

Many Catholic leaders and clergy were quick to criticize the decision. Father George Tavard blasted the Pope in the *National Catholic Reporter*. Father Bernard Häring of Rome, widely regarded as the leading moral theologian at the time, called upon Catholic women and men to follow their consciences, rather than the Pope's decree.[15] When the Pope issued his encyclical, large numbers of American Catholics had already made up their own minds. By 1965, three out of four Catholics believed that anyone who wanted contraceptives should have access to them, and more than half had used them. The percentages were even higher in other countries. Soon, American Catholic women would be taking the pill at the same rate as non-Catholics. By the end of the decade, many American and western European priests were openly giving their married parishioners permission to use contraceptives, in defiance of the Pope's decree.[16]

Although the Pope affirmed the ban, which continues to this day, the pill contributed to profound changes in the relationship between Church leaders, clergy, and lay members. After Vatican II, which opened the way for greater empowerment and expression of dissenting views among both clergy and laity, Catholic women and men increasingly consulted their consciences, in addition to Church teachings, for guidance in their personal decisions. One Catholic husband, frustrated by the rhythm method, decided in 1969 to reject the Church's teachings: "I'm sick of this S.O.S. (Sex On Schedule) routine. How can the church expect a couple to turn sex on and off like a light switch? Sexual relations should be guided by love, by emotion, by need and not by a schedule and not by one negative vote from Rome."[17]

John Rock was the most visible of the practicing Catholics whose conscience led him to boldly reject the Church's teachings, but he was not alone. Birth control had been driving a wedge between Catholics and Church leaders even before the pill arrived. The timing of the pill's arrival, and its acceptance among Catholics, widened that chasm. The pill weakened the power of the papacy in the lives of Catholics, and after *Humanae Vitae*, turned many Catholics away from the Church altogether.

WHILE CHURCH AUTHORITIES FACED DISSENT, PRESSURE began to mount against medical experts. In the 1950s and early 1960s, it seemed that medical research could do no wrong. Miracle drugs like the polio vaccine, mild tranquilizers, and oral contraceptives seemed to offer a better and safer life for all. These new drugs promised healthy individuals peace of mind: no more fears of the dreaded polio, no more anxieties in the new atomic age, no more fears of unwanted pregnancy. Americans embraced these medical breakthroughs with unbridled enthusiasm.[18] But as time went on, these miracle drugs began to seem less miraculous and more dangerous.

Tranquilizers were a case in point. When Miltown appeared on the market in 1955, it became an instant blockbuster. Within a year, one in every twenty Americans had tried it. Other tranquilizers quickly entered the market, including Librium and Valium in the 1960s. But soon it became obvious that these were not harmless drugs—rather, they were seriously addicting. "Mother's little helpers" were trapping thousands of Americans, including large numbers of suburban housewives, in dependence and addiction.[19]

The most horrifying tranquilizer tragedy resulted from thalidomide, a drug developed to calm the frayed nerves of anxious adults and to alleviate morning sickness in pregnant women. Thalidomide was developed in Germany and sold widely throughout Europe, but the FDA never granted approval for it to be marketed in the United States, thanks to the persistence of Dr. Frances Oldham Kelsey. The mother of two children and one of the few woman doctors working for the agency, Kelsey joined the FDA as a reviewer in August 1960. With a master's degree in pharmacology from McGill University and M.D. and Ph.D. degrees from the University of Chicago, she was well prepared for the task of evaluating new pharmaceutical products. She also had a particular interest in drugs and fetal safety, a topic she had studied as a graduate student. One month after Kelsey took the job at the FDA, William S. Merrell, Inc., applied for approval to sell thalidomide in the United States. The drug was so popular in Europe that its FDA approval was expected to be quick and routine. The task of evaluating its safety fell to Kelsey. Kelsey was not convinced that the drug was safe, especially for pregnant women. She asked the company to submit additional data, which it did. But she remained unconvinced.

Officials from Merrell tried in vain to persuade Kelsey to approve the drug, but she stood her ground, even when they complained to her superiors that she was stubborn and unreasonable. She later explained that she had expected "to get bullied and pressured by industry," and that she would need to resist such intimidating tactics. Merrell sent its application forward six times over the next two years. As Merrell pushed for approval, thousands of women in Europe who had taken it during pregnancy, and a small number of American women who had gained access to the drug, gave birth to "thalidomide babies" lacking limbs and with other catastrophic birth defects. In 1961 German officials took thalidomide off the market, and the following year Merrell withdrew its FDA application. Kelsey became a national hero for preventing the drug from being marketed in the United States. Her actions earned her the medal for Distinguished Federal Civilian Service, awarded by President Kennedy.[20]

Just as Americans were learning of the thalidomide disaster unfolding in Europe, problems began to surface with the oral contraceptive. The first report of thrombosis in a woman on the pill came in 1961. A year later there were twenty-six reports of women who developed blood clots while taking the pill, six of whom had died.[21] It was difficult to determine whether or not the pill caused thrombosis, because there was no way to know how many women in the general population were afflicted. Eventually it became clear that women on the pill were at higher risk for blood clots. Soon, other health concerns surfaced. Did the pill increase or decrease the risk of certain cancers? What about other side effects, such as headaches, nausea, weight gain, and depression?

Some doctors and pill advocates, including Gregory Pincus, made light of the side effects and minimized the dangers, insisting that the vast majority of women on the pill had no serious problems. But for the women who suffered from them, the statistics were cold comfort. Several early users of the pill described in a survey their experiences when the oral contraceptive still contained high doses of hormones. Aurora M took the pill as a teenager in the 1960s to regulate her periods, but it made her sick with vomiting, diarrhea, and headaches. These symptoms were not minor nuisances. "The pill hurt me more than helped me, I never tried to use anything else, afraid it might cause more damage to me."[22] The harm to Jenny S was even worse. As a Catholic, she did not take the pill until after her fifth child was born. Two weeks later she had a massive stroke that left her paralyzed on the left side of her body. She remained in a coma for several weeks before being transferred to a rehabilitation hospital for several months, while her parents moved into her home to care for her children. She returned home in a wheelchair. Her daughter recalled, "The impact on the family was total devastation, both emotionally and financially. . . . None of us came out unscarred, and the effects are lasting."[23]

Even women who had no problems themselves worried about the health risks of the pill. Ilene W took the pill as a teenager in the 1960s. Her father was a doctor who warned her about such drugs. "I remember him being so worried that he was seeing broken blood vessels in the eyes of young women taking these high-dose pills. . . . One of my friends did have a stroke shortly after her marriage that was attributed to the pill." Ilene W joined a women's group that brought in a female doctor to discuss the risks of the pill. She eventually switched to a diaphragm. At the age of fifty-eight, Ilene got breast cancer.[24] Although there was no evidence that the pill was a causal factor, she couldn't help but wonder.

WITHIN A FEW YEARS OF THE PILL'S FDA APPROVAL, women began demanding information and answers. Initially, the pill was approved at a hormone dosage of 10 milligrams. Researchers were not sure that a lower-dose pill would be effective, so the 10-milligram pill was the only one that was tested and approved. When studies showed that lower-dose pills were equally effective, researchers and pharmaceutical companies began to reduce the amount of hormones contained in each pill, which cut down on the dangers and side effects. Yet questions, doubts, and risks persisted. By the end of the decade, the pill had lost its glow as a miracle drug. In 1969, as the feminist movement gained momentum, journalist Barbara Seaman heated up the controversy with her book *The Doctors' Case Against the Pill*.[25]

Barbara Seaman had an established career as a writer for women's magazines. In the early 1960s, she and her psychiatrist husband, Dr. Gideon Seaman, wrote a column for *Brides* magazine on marriage, and she later wrote for *Ladies Home Journal* and *Family Circle*. By the late 1960s she had become an advocate for women's health. In *The Doctors' Case Against the Pill*, she supported her case with the opinions of physicians who shared her views, and she insisted that ordinary women taking the pill were unaware of "the disenchantment and dismay that are increasingly disturbing the inner councils of the medical profession."[26] The book included reports of research on health risks such as blood clots and provided doctors' testimonies regarding a host of other dangers and side effects. It also contained numerous stories of individual women who developed serious complications while taking the pill. Seaman argued that women needed to have access to all the information about the pill's risks and dangers. Highly critical of the pill and the authorities who promoted it, she called upon women to take charge of their own medical decisions.

But in Seaman's effort to marshal all experts she could find to support her case against the pill, she unwittingly collaborated with some who had their own agendas. The worst offender in this regard was Hugh Davis, a researcher eager to denounce the pill and promote his own invention, the Dalkon Shield intrauterine device (IUD). Later, when the infamous Dalkon Shield caused thousands of women to suffer severe harm and even death, Davis's true motives became evident. He owned a one-third share in the company that marketed the Dalkon Shield, and he had falsified data from his studies of the device. But when Barbara Seaman wrote her book, none of this had come to light. In fact, Davis wrote the introduction to Seaman's book. He warned against the dangers of the pill and promoted the Dalkon Shield, but neither he nor Seaman questioned the safety of his IUD, from which he stood to profit handsomely.[27]

The Doctors' Case Against the Pill failed to avert the Dalkon Shield catastrophe and very likely contributed to it. Davis used the platform provided by Barbara Seaman to promote his flawed product. From 1971 until 1974, when its manufacturer, A.H. Robins, withdrew it from the market because of complaints about its safety, 2.2 million women had been fitted with the Dalkon Shield—more than all other IUDs combined. At least 18 women died as a result of the device, and more than 200,000 women suffered infections, hysterectomies, miscarriages, and other serious problems or had children with birth defects. More than 325,000 claims were filed against A.H. Robins. The company went bankrupt in 1985.[28]

At the time Seaman published her book, however, the pill was the focus of attention. Among the readers who found her book persuasive was Senator Gaylord Nelson, long a critic of big business and the pharmaceutical industry in particular. Nelson called for hearings on the oral contraceptive, which began in January 1970. Several of Seaman's sources testified, beginning with Hugh Davis, who condemned the pill as unsafe and touted the safety and efficacy of his IUD. He deceived the committee about his financial interest in the Dalkon Shield, insisting he had none. *Time* reported that among the witnesses called to testify, critics of the pill outnumbered defenders by seven to one.[29]

The hearings gained huge publicity. Although women's health advocates were gratified that the Senate was considering the safety of the pill, they were enraged that no women were called to testify. Not even Barbara Seaman testified. Infuriated, the feminist group D.C. Women's Liberation disrupted the hearings with protests that were captured by news cameras and broadcast across the nation. But none of the women were given an opportunity to speak at the hearings, even though it was women who had prompted the investigation, and their outrage at being excluded from the proceedings gained them additional coverage in the press. Although barred from testifying, women had a considerable impact on the outcome.

By 1970, the FDA ordered manufacturers to include in every packet of the pills an information sheet detailing the side effects and health risks. The hearings also affected women's behavior: 18 percent of women who had been on the pill stopped taking it in the aftermath of the hearings and the attendant media coverage. Within a few months, the percentage of pill takers returned to its previous level, but women continued to pressure doctors and drug companies to improve it.[30] In response to complaints that the initial package inserts were incomplete and difficult for non-physicians to decipher, eventually drug companies provided more user-friendly information materials.

In spite of improvements in dosage and packaging, questions persisted about the pill's safety, and feminists kept up the pressure. In 1977, for example, a televised debate on the *David Susskind Show* brought together a group of physicians and scientists to debate the safety and efficacy of the pill. Barbara Seaman was the sole woman on the panel. All the men with one exception defended the pill's safety record, while Seaman, struggling to get a word in edgewise, raised objections. The scientists on the panel described the thorough research that had been conducted on the pill, its new and safer lower dose, and its record of success. The doctors said they would not hesitate to prescribe the pill to the women in their families and indeed had done so. Nevertheless, David Susskind, moderating the debate, turned to the studio audience for comments by those who had suffered harm while taking the pill, including a man whose wife had died from a blood clot. Susskind said he would never want anyone in his family to take the pill, and he asked the men on the panel, "Why the hell would you recommend the pill?"

After the panelists confronted Susskind, he backed away from his condemnation of the pill and instead encouraged viewers to consult their doctors before making a decision on what contraceptive was best for them. In spite of Susskind's final concession and the reassuring words of most of the scientists on the panel, the emotional weight of the program was on the side of Seaman and the pill's other critics, who brought their powerful personal stories of suffering to the broadcast.[31]

Seaman was among the founders of the broad-based women's health movement. In Boston, a group of women began meeting informally to learn about women's health care issues and to teach a course in the local community. The group became the Boston Women's Health Book Collective (BWHBC), the most visible and influential voice of the women's health movement. The group's signature accomplishment was its 1973 publication of *Our Bodies, Ourselves*, which sold nearly 4 million copies and was translated into twelve languages.[32]

Like Margaret Sanger and Katharine McCormick, the members of the BWHBC were activists intensely concerned about women's reproductive rights. But that is where the similarities ended. Had the two early pioneers lived into the 1970s, they might have been dismayed to see so many of their basic principles abandoned by the next feminist generation. While

Sanger and McCormick wanted a pill that would be totally in the control of women, the BWHBC called for continued research into a male pill. While Sanger and McCormick insisted on prescriptions for contraceptives and frequent medical examinations, the BWHBC distrusted doctors and encouraged women to examine themselves. Sanger and McCormick urged pharmaceutical companies to develop and market contraceptives to meet women's needs, but the BWHBC saw the pharmaceutical industry as interested only in making money, often at the expense of women's health. The BWHBC claimed that capitalist medicine was "no more dedicated to improving the people's health than . . . General Motors [is] to improving people's public transportation."[33]

Over time, the women's health movement shifted its position on the pill. The first edition of *Our Bodies, Ourselves* took a neutral position, noting that the pill was dangerous for some women but that many used it with no problems at all. The authors urged their readers to make an informed decision about whether or not the pill was right for them.[34] In later editions of the book, the BWHBC became less confident about the pill. In 1976, the authors advised caution, noting that after only fifteen years on the market its long-term effects had not yet been demonstrated. By 1984, the authors were even skeptical of the pill's effectiveness: "Some of us choose to take whatever risks are involved because we *falsely* believe we are getting 100 percent effectiveness and absolutely don't want to become pregnant. What price do we pay for this *alleged* perfect protection?"[35] The 1998 edition no longer supported the pill and instead recommended the diaphragm, cervical cap, or foam and condom, with abortion as a backup in case of failure. "We must try to change the attitudes and prejudices that have kept us from using these methods in the past."[36] Sanger and McCormick might have been rolling in their graves at these pronouncements.

By 2005, however, the movement's perspective had come full circle to a resounding endorsement of the pill. The authors of *Our Bodies, Ourselves: A New Edition for a New Era* noted that the pill now contained a mere fraction of the hormones that in larger doses had caused so many risks and side effects. They cautioned readers to reject "alarming stories from friends, trusted adults, or the media. . . . These stories may be based on half-truths, isolated cases, or old information." Encouraging their readers to base their decisions on accurate information, they hailed the benefits of oral contraceptives: "The advent of the Pill, probably more than any other event, has enabled women the world over to prevent or delay pregnancy and, in doing so, to complete our educations, choose our careers, and create more egalitarian relationships. . . . The birth control pill is considered the most intensely researched medication in history. . . . Despite problems associated with early pill formulations, researchers now maintain that the low-dose birth control pills on the market today are safe for most women."[37] Sanger and McCormick could rest in peace.

WHILE THE TURMOIL SURROUNDING THE PILL SUBSIDED in the waning years of the twentieth century, new controversies emerged with the next generation of hormonal contraceptives, particularly Norplant, a long-acting compound implanted in the upper arm, and Depo Provera, an injectable contraceptive that prevented pregnancy for three to six months. Norplant gained FDA approval in 1990 and Depo Provera in 1992. Both of these methods had the advantage of protection against pregnancy without the need to remember to take a pill every day.

Hailed as the first new contraceptive in three decades and touted as more effective and easier to use than the pill, Norplant consisted of six flexible, silicone-based capsules, each containing 36 milligrams of continually released hormones, preventing pregnancy for up to five years. It was first developed in the late 1960s, and within a decade the Population Council was testing it in developing countries, prior to its approval for use in the United States. More than 50,000 women in forty-four countries took part in studies that yielded hundreds of articles in medical journals. The World Health Organization followed 8,000 users for five years, comparing them to women who used the IUD or sterilization, and found that Norplant users had fewer problems. Finland and Sweden approved Norplant in the 1980s. By the time the FDA approved Norplant for use in the United States, nearly 5 million women around the world had used it. The main drawback to Norplant was the fact that it required a physician to remove it. Women couldn't remove it themselves. For that reason, providers of Norplant had an ethical responsibility to make sure that women had access to trained medical personnel who could remove the device on demand.[38]

The inability of women to insert or remove the device themselves left open the possibility of coercive use, especially in the 1990s when the political climate grew hostile to welfare and some taxpayers complained about public support for the children of women on public assistance. When the FDA approved Norplant for use in the United States, almost immediately the new device generated a storm of controversy. The *Philadelphia Inquirer* set off a firestorm with an editorial that promoted Norplant as a means to "reduce the underclass" and urged financial incentives for inner-city black women on welfare. The public outcry was intense. *Inquirer* columnist Steve Lopez fumed at his colleague's suggestion that "black people should be paid to stop having so many damn kids," and the paper printed an apology.[39]

Nevertheless, the idea took hold. Policymakers and pundits across the country saw Norplant as a means to curb the fertility of poor women, particularly those on welfare. Numerous legislative proposals attempted to require Norplant for women who used drugs, or who had more than a certain number of children on public assistance. Dr. Sheldon Segal, one of the scientists who developed Norplant, was enraged. He condemned these proposals, asserting that Norplant "was developed to improve reproductive freedom, not to restrict it."[40]

A Republican congressman from Florida, however, suggested a federal program linking welfare to the use of Norplant. A state judge in California offered a woman convicted of child abuse the choice of Norplant or prison. Advocates for such programs included black as well as white policymakers. Marion Barry, an African American who was mayor of Washington, D.C., supported the idea: "You can have as many babies as you want," he said. "But when you start asking the government to take care of them, the government now ought to have some control over you."[41]

No state ever passed a bill that mandated the use of Norplant or offered financial incentives for using it. But many poor women and teenage girls found that it was easier and cheaper to acquire than other forms of birth control. Although Norplant was expensive when administered through private doctors, it was offered for free through subsidized clinics and in predominantly black public schools. There is no question that Norplant was more effective than the pill for preventing pregnancy among teens. One study found that only 2 percent of adolescents became pregnant while using Norplant, compared to 38 percent who used the pill. But the practice of distributing Norplant to teenagers remained controversial.[42]

By the late 1990s, Norplant fell out of favor as a result of several class-action suits against the manufacturers. In 1997, out of 1 million American women using Norplant, 25,000 of them—one in a thousand—had signed on to 200 lawsuits claiming that they had been injured by the product. Most claimed that they had permanent scarring from the insertion or removal of the implant. Fifty of these were class-action suits, some generated by lawyers who placed ads with toll-free numbers offering money to women using Norplant. Ironically, the manufacturers of Norplant had developed a biodegradable form of the implant that would not need to be removed. But women's health groups vigorously opposed the biodegradable product because it could not be removed if a woman decided she no longer wanted the implant.[43]

Although lawyers for the manufacturer, Wyeth-Ayerst, successfully defended Norplant, negative publicity continued, and in 1999 the manufacturer agreed to a settlement. After spending $40 million defending Norplant, the company discontinued production in 2002. Norplant's use in the United States declined, although it remained popular in other countries. Newer products have reduced the number of implanted tubes, making insertion and removal easier.[44]

In the United States, many of the controversies surrounding contraceptives have resulted in lawsuits where experts and authorities have battled against each other on behalf of either consumers or manufacturers. Some of these legal actions were important and well deserved, especially the litigation against the Dalkon Shield. But some researchers believe that the numerous lawsuits have inhibited the development of new contraceptive products in the United States, mainly because of the huge costs of liability insurance.[45] By the 1980s, in the United States, there were more liability suits for oral contraceptives than for any other category of drug—so many that liability insurance was temporarily unavailable. Legal challenges to contraceptive products continued into the twenty-first century.[46]

In addition to the liability problem, regulations that required lengthy testing discouraged investment in contraceptive innovations. The cost of research and development for new contraceptives also soared. Gradually, as U.S. pharmaceutical companies withdrew from contraceptive development, researchers came to rely on government funding. Research continued in Europe, where there were fewer lawsuits.[47] Nevertheless, in Europe as well as in the United States, measures put into place to protect consumers had the unintended result of limiting the number and variety of contraceptive products available to men as well as women.[48]

American women have become discerning consumers of birth control products, largely as a result of the efforts of feminists and women's health care advocates to improve the safety and accessibility of the pill and other contraceptives. Today, women in their childbearing years encounter many new contraceptive products, a very different sexual culture, and transformed medical and pharmaceutical institutions. They have vastly greater control over their reproductive lives than their mothers had. Yet as they tell their stories, we find that while much has changed, much has also remained the same.

7

The Pill Today

I love the pill!

Susan G, age 26

The pill sucks!

Carol O, age 29[1]

The quotes above express the extremes of young women's feelings toward the pill today. Although it is not for everyone, the pill remains the leading contraceptive of choice in the United States. Much has changed since it first came on the market. Women have more birth control options, more life choices and opportunities, and increased equality in private and public life. There is more openness and acceptance regarding sexual activity for single and married women, and less stigma surrounding unwed sex and pregnancy. The pill is a much safer product than it was in 1960, and women face fewer legal obstacles to obtaining contraception and abortion. Yet the pill is still an imperfect contraceptive, and women still encounter roadblocks on the path to full reproductive freedom.

Today nearly 12 million women in the United States take the pill. More than 45 million women of childbearing age have taken the pill at some point in their lives. Unlike their mothers who saw the pill as a miraculous godsend, many young women today take the pill for granted. As Anne S commented, "The pill seems so commonplace. It's like asking what the impact of the telephone system is. It's so ubiquitous, I just couldn't picture a fully functioning society without it!"[2] For Alice Z it is "such a common part of my everyday routine (like brushing my teeth). . . . It's a non-issue."[3] Elizabeth M appreciated her choices: "It's just a question of which contraceptive options are the most fun and the least hassle."[4]

Nevertheless, many realize that access to the pill is a luxury that was not available to women of an earlier generation and that its impact has been monumental. Martha L considers the pill "the single most empowering option that women have been given in all of history."[5] For Kelly R, the pill is more than an effective contraceptive: "[It] helped me to own my identity as a woman and to be in control of my life, my body, and my future."[6] Jessica P feels like "one of the lucky women in the world. To be born in the United States, and to be born after the pill was available, I have never been forced to have children, or been forced to abort because I never had an opportunity to protect myself. I've been able to live the life I wanted to lead. And most importantly, I've never had to rely on the consent or willingness of my partner in order to protect myself. It's all been in my hands. I think that's huge, and I'm grateful for it every day."[7]

These women all responded to an Internet query asking for opinions, experiences, and stories about the pill.[8] They had little in common. Anne S, age twenty-one, describes herself as "married, bisexual, ex-military, living below the poverty line." Alice Z, age thirty, married, white, and straight, a self-described atheist and a Democrat, is from a poor, working-class, fundamentalist Christian small-town family. She and her sisters are first-generation pill users and the first in their family to attend college. Mary M is a twenty-three-year-old aeronautical engineer for a company that makes jet fighters. What these women do have in common, along with more than a hundred others, is that they all had something they wanted to say about the pill, so they wrote their stories for inclusion in this book. What they tell us reflects the many ways in which the pill has been at the center of the major transformations in women's lives over the last half century—how much has changed and how much has remained the same.

The feminist movement expanded women's opportunities, altered relations between the sexes, and challenged social, legal, and institutional structures. The entire context in which women approach sex, relationships, contraception, and reproduction has changed dramatically. Women today have a different relationship to the pill than their mothers had. Yet at the same time, young women grapple with some of the same issues that faced their mothers, as well as some new ones. Dilemmas and difficulties remain for women seeking to control their fertility.

The first generation of pill takers felt liberated by its effectiveness and trusted it to prevent pregnancy more than other contraceptives available at the time. Today, many young women use a barrier method along with the pill, either because they don't consider the pill to be 100 percent effective or because it does not protect against sexually transmitted diseases. Although she takes the pill, Melissa G and her boyfriend "still use condoms, but only right before climax to keep down on mess and that pesky 2 percent noneffectiveness."[9] Samantha J, age twenty-three, never had any trouble with the pill, "but I always use a condom as well, just in case. I guess I'm still a little nervous!"[10]

Many women today recognize that the pill has played a role in their sexual autonomy as well as their reproductive self-determination. "I think it's hard enough, even for those of us raised feminist, for women to ask for what they want in sex and sexual relationships," noted Jessica P. "Having to add negotiations about birth control on top of that power imbalance just tips the scale even more. Taking back our control of our bodies in terms of birth control really helps women to take the leap to be open and honest and ask for what we want in bed. . . . The pill has helped me feel less dependent on my male partners, and more equal with them."

In addition to her sexual assertiveness, Jessica P also identified herself in ways that would have been rare among her mother's peers: a thirty-eight-year-old lawyer, married, non-monogamous, and bisexual.[11] In the 1960s, relatively few married women would have been lawyers, few wives would have admitted being nonmonogamous, and few pill users would have identified themselves as bisexual. Nearly all pill users at the time identified as heterosexual; lesbians would have been highly unlikely to use the pill. Today women are more likely to embrace a sexual identity that is more complex. Among the respondents to the Internet query, about 10 percent identified themselves as bisexual. For some, bisexuality raised new issues regarding the pill. Karen E explained, "The only problem with relationships . . . was that when I was dating a girl and taking the pill, she assumed that meant I was likely to cheat on her with a guy! It played into the whole stereotype of bi girls as promiscuous and always looking for a guy to screw on the side."[12]

Along with sexual identity, expectations for sexual pleasure have also evolved since the 1960s. When the pill first arrived on the market, many women reported that it both freed them from fear of pregnancy and allowed for a spontaneity unavailable with barrier methods, making sex more enjoyable. In striking contrast, among the young women today who responded to the Internet query, several complained that the pill actually lowered their libido. Available data suggest that the pill can either increase or decrease libido—but most women are not presented with this information. Few doctors explain to their patients that the pill can lessen the sex drive in some women. Manufacturers rarely mention it in their information packets. For example, the full product information for Ortho Tri-Cyclin Lo contains a long list of possible side effects in the fine print, and another list of reported side effects that have been "neither confirmed nor refuted," which included "changes in libido."[13] Internet sites including WebMD and Teens Health do not mention lowered libido as a possible side effect.[14] However, other Web sites, such as Epigee Women's

Health, note, "New research now indicates that the birth control pill may inhibit more than just pregnancy. The pill may also significantly, and perhaps permanently, dampen your sexual drive."[15]

Several of the young women respondents spoke to their friends and female relatives about the effects of the pill on their libido and did their own research on the Internet. Mandy B learned that "many of the women in my life had also started to react negatively to the pill after many years. For example, we all shared a decreased sex drive. How could it be that the same pill that liberated my sexual self was also now changing my feelings about sex? I didn't feel like me."[16] When Helen P took the pill at age eighteen, "I realized it had sucked my sex drive away. I loved the spontaneity of it, compared to condoms, and the security of it, but it got to the point where I was never interested in sex." She bypassed her health providers, who dismissed her complaints of depression and lowered libido, and went to the Internet. "After some online research, I realized I wasn't alone in this symptom—nobody had ever told me it was possible— and I went off the pill."[17] Valerie J was "very sad that a pill that is supposed to make sex easier and safer also makes it less desirable." Her boyfriend "took it as a rejection, that I didn't find him attractive, even suggested I might be a lesbian (gasp!)."[18] Barbara E simply "hated the pill. It wrecked my body, gave me headaches and eradicated my libido. I suppose that's another way to prevent pregnancy—having no desire to have sex."[19] Sally G complained, "Holy Hell. Can you even imagine if a birth control medication for men blunted their libido? There'd be outrage. No no, there wouldn't, because no drug like that would be taken by millions of men for most of their lives."[20] (Her observation, of course, is correct.)

Although today's pill may not suppress libido more than the original oral contraceptive did, women today may well experience the effects of the pill differently. For many in the first generation of pill users, the intense fear of pregnancy diminished women's libido to such an extent that when they went on the pill and that fear disappeared, their sexual pleasure increased considerably. Today there is no longer the terror of facing an illegal abortion, a ruined reputation, banishment to a home for unwed mothers, or a hasty marriage. With legal abortion, the "morning-after pill," and the easing of the stigma against unwed pregnancy, women have more options and the stakes are not as high. Moreover, today's young women are more likely to be in tune with their sexuality than those in their mothers' generation were, many of whom experienced sex outside of marriage as secret and shameful, and only came to know their bodies over time within marriage. The sexual revolution opened up more discussion about sex, and the feminist movement encouraged women to explore and enjoy their own sexuality. With so many contraceptive options available to women today, some are unwilling to compromise their sexual pleasure for the convenience of the pill. On the other hand, not all women on the pill experience this side effect. According to one report, "As for libido, while some studies show a decreased sex drive, others show an increase." Just as in their mothers' day, "a lower chance of pregnancy can be quite an aphrodisiac."[21]

Clearly, the sexual revolution and the feminist movement have had a huge impact on sexual behavior, values, expectations, and mores. Even so, the double standard, parental disapproval, shame, fear, and secrecy surrounding sex still persist. Susan G explained that as a student from a conservative Southern family, "I lived in fear of getting pregnant, mainly because it would mean my father knowing I was having premarital sex and that he would disown me." She went on the pill when she married, and stayed on it after she divorced. Today, the twenty-six-year-old chemical engineer reflects on her contraceptive use: "I think the impact of the pill on my sex life is that it allows me to have one."[22]

Katie M's path to the pill was even more fraught. She "never worked up the nerve to visit the gynecologist and ask them, or anyone else, about birth control. In fact, I was the perfect statistic—a product of an abstinence-only sex/health education that only led me to withhold sexual activity slightly longer than average and prevented me from using birth control because that would imply I had been *planning* on having sex, heaven forbid." So she and her boyfriend began having unprotected sex. "I hated myself so much. I hated myself for not speaking up about what I knew was irresponsible sexual behavior." When she and her partner decided to use condoms, that too was an ordeal. "Having both been virgins and both completely embarrassed about sex (that we denied we were having), we spent about six seconds furtively looking at the condom display in Wal-Mart before randomly picking a package. Even though I knew the proper way to put a condom on thanks to the Internet, I was too paralyzed by shame and guilt about having sex in the first place (an obvious sign I shouldn't have gone that far since I wasn't personally comfortable with it) to properly apply it. I'm pretty sure we bought the wrong size as well. Needless to say, the condom broke just as he came inside of me for the first time. I ended up with a strangely soul-numbing yet panicky pregnancy scare and that was probably the beginning of the end of my first relationship."

Katie faced her own guilt as well as parental disapproval. "The crazy thing is that I never even considered the pill. Between my parents, my religious upbringing, and poor sexual education I was under the impression that girls that used the pill were sluts. Even if I had wondered about getting birth control, I felt I couldn't visit a gynecologist because my mother would somehow find out I had been having sex and lose all trust in me. Or be really disappointed." She could not even turn to her college health center, or to her friends. "There was no way I could talk to my school nurse, since I attended a Christian college. I suspected that I would probably be investigated and expelled or 'campused' if someone found out. I couldn't bear the thought of my friends finding out either. I was so afraid of losing their respect and becoming 'dirty' in their eyes that I deliberately avoided looking suspicious." Finally, in her junior year, she attended a free seminar on women's health that transformed her attitudes about sex and birth control. "I researched the various types of birth control and realized how many options I had. As my sexual education expanded, I stumbled into feminism and began to realize just how many choices the pill affords me." Taking control of her sexuality and fertility led her to feminism—rather than the other way around. "I would never stay with a man who would presume to dictate what I did with my body and sexual health.

I also realized just how stupidly lucky I had been that I had never become pregnant after having unprotected sex for over a year. . . . I ended my college career older, wiser, and much better off emotionally."[23]

Katie M was one of several Internet respondents who sought help from health professionals when they felt unable to turn to family or friends. Jenny B did the same. She began taking the pill at age fifteen. In her small town in north Florida, "everyone was nominally to extremely religious and both sex and birth control were considered to be an 'after-marriage-only' option." But her town also had a high teen pregnancy rate. Knowing that Jenny's family would disapprove, a nurse at the medical office where she worked gave her the pills for free. "I had to keep them hidden from my parents."[24]

Like Jenny B, nearly half of the Internet respondents began taking the pill as young teenagers. The most common age was sixteen, but some were younger. The youngest was eleven when she first took the pill to control heavy bleeding. Although there is no available data for how many first-generation pill takers were unmarried when they first took the pill, or the age at which they began, young single women of the 1960s faced legal barriers, medical hostility, parental disapproval, and their own ethical qualms. Today's teens are less likely to encounter those inhibiting factors. Some of the respondents first took the pill to alleviate severe menstrual symptoms and discovered its contraceptive benefits soon after they began taking it.

A few young women acknowledged that the pill had a negative effect on their sexual behavior. Kristy H confessed, "The pill became an easy way out for me to engage in promiscuous sexual activity, and a form of abuse. I would take it straight through for months at a time so as to miss my period and be able to have sex 'like a man.' Now that I'm off of it completely, I feel more in control."[25] Melissa B also felt that the pill led her down a path to irresponsible sex and only later to a process of growth and responsibility. She began taking the pill at age fifteen, and remembers "the power this gave me over my sexuality and the liberty I felt to be a sexual human being." But she also saw the pill "as a 'free card' to sexual activity. . . . All the same, the pill was still there as a silent partner, as my perceptions of myself as a sexual being continued to grow and be challenged into adulthood."[26]

These accounts make it clear that in spite of feminism and the sexual revolution, some women experience the same guilt, shame, and parental disapproval that faced their mothers' generation. For some of them, the pill was part of a path not only to responsible contraception, but also to new ideas about sex, greater personal empowerment, and feminist identity. Other young women had no need to break away from parental attitudes because their parents were supportive and encouraging. When Carrie R was heading off to college, her father, a family physician, urged her to go on the pill. "It was his opinion that it was much simpler to start on the pill then, before I was sexually active, than to wait until after I needed contraception. . . . It was rather a weird conversation to have with my Dad, me being the really innocent sixteen-year-old homeschooled girl that I was. However, as soon as I got to university I went down to the health clinic and got a prescription."[27]

Many of the young women who had the support of their parents were raised by feminist mothers. Linda L was one such woman. "I have been a feminist since I was ten years old, and the magazines I would read growing up (*Seventeen*, *YM*, *Sassy*, etc.) always touted birth control as a positive thing. When I started dating, my mother told me to 'use protection.' I'm extremely grateful for our feminist foremothers who made it possible for us to have access to birth control without there being too much of a stigma."[28] Erika B's mother, an ob/gyn nurse, got her Norplant when she was fifteen, because she felt it was more reliable and long term for a teenager.[29] Carolyn P began taking the pill at age sixteen. "After [I told] my Mom I was interested in being sexually active with my boyfriend at the time, she insisted I get on the pill."[30] Anita K reported, "When it comes to ethics or morals I have never thought twice about using birth control. My grandmother had my mother when she was barely sixteen and was forced into a miserable marriage right before my mother was born, so I have grown up with strong women telling me to make my own choices about my body. In high school, my mom was the mom who took my friends to the clinic to get birth control, since they were scared of their own mothers' reactions to their sexuality."[31]

Clearly, there is a wide range of attitudes toward sex and contraception in the generations since the pill became available. There is also a wide range of experiences with side effects. In spite of the vast improvements in oral contraceptives over the last half century and the wide array of hormonal contraceptives now available, many young women on the pill today suffer the same symptoms that plagued their mothers' generation. Julie D expressed the sentiments of many when she said that the pill was "the most miserable thing I've ever put into my body."[32]

Some described severe psychological and emotional effects. Jane B took the once-a-month injection, and each time, "two days later I was an absolute emotional wreck. Paranoia, depression, anger, it was horrible." Carol O said the pill turned her into "a raving lunatic." Melissa G suffered severe nausea and vomiting, so she tried the low-dose pill but "bled constantly the entire time, and often woke up with headaches that pain killers would not relieve."[33] Kristol R reported that the pill caused a friend of hers to be so "depressed and listless" that it took two years away from her life. For Kristol R, however, the pill was a blessing: "I haven't told her this, but while the pill might have taken two years of her life, the pill gave me my life."[34]

Side effects did not trouble every woman taking the pill. In fact, some reported taking it for its noncontraceptive benefits. Several respondents took the pill because it provides control over inconvenient bodily functions, particularly menstruation. Some went on the pill to eliminate their periods altogether. Initially, manufacturers of the oral contraceptives presumed that women would object to a pill that eliminated the monthly period. But some women welcome this effect.[35] They skip the "placebo pills" of the fourth week in the pill packet so they can avoid having a fake period. Robyn E "found the pill to be invaluable. I actually take it all the time; I know that the manufacturers say that you should leave the seven-day gap, but I can't see any reason to because any 'period' you get is just withdrawal bleeding anyway. . . . I don't feel any sort of earthy link with my cycle; to be honest I'd be perfectly happy if it just went away. Then again, I don't intend to have children."[36]

Mary M, a twenty-three-year-old engineer, raved about the pill: "More than contraception, it is a way to control my period. . . . It has so many other fantastic side effects! . . . I can have my period whenever I want. If I don't want to have my period ever again, I don't have to. If I want to take a beach vacation or have sex with my boyfriend, I can. I am in control of my body."[37] Linda O appreciated other side effects. On the pill since age seventeen, she "really can't say enough good things about it. It cleared up most of my acne, made my breasts bigger, and lessened my menstrual cramps. What's not to love?"[38]

Letty C found the pill to be "incredibly liberating. I studied abroad in college and the pill made it possible for me to skip my periods entirely during my travel abroad . . . which was a huge benefit, and since then I have used the sneaky period-skip method to avoid having a period on a number of other highly inconvenient occasions (during final exams, vacations, on my birthday, etc.)."[39]

Jane D had more professional reasons for wanted to control her cycle. As a woman in the military, she began taking the pill shortly after joining the Army and used it for nine years to regulate her period. She faced situations that would have been unthinkable for women of her mother's generation. "Before the pill, I never knew when my period would come. I didn't know how long it would be, or how heavy. My job in the military required me to work in remote areas. . . . We lived in tents, used port-a-johns, and got showers every three days or once a week, depending on our resources. We would do this for weeks or months. This was our job. . . . I needed to know when my periods would come and what they would be like. I didn't want to bleed through my clothes. There were very few women in my field and I knew that I would be looked at as an example of what all women in the military would be like. I would not be viewed as an individual. The pill was invaluable."[40] As Jane D's experience demonstrates, new opportunities that opened up for women led to unanticipated benefits of the pill.

Pharmaceutical companies realized that some women took the pill for its beneficial side effects, rather than primarily for contraception. In 2009, Bayer Health Care Pharmaceuticals advertised the noncontraceptive benefits of Yaz, the most popular birth control pill in the United States. Because Yaz was approved only as an oral contraceptive, the FDA forced Bayer to launch a $20 million advertising campaign to counter its previous claims that Yaz would cure acne or premenstrual symptoms. The FDA ruled that the original ads were misleading and encouraged women to take the drug for purposes other than contraception. Nevertheless, some women continued to take the pill for its noncontraceptive benefits.[41]

Another unexpected effect of the pill was its contribution to increasing openness regarding matters of sex, reproduction, and contraception. Open communication enhanced women's relationships with the men in their lives, their female friends, and their health care providers. In the pill's early years, it contributed to greater communication between doctors and their female patients. As the sexual revolution and the feminist movement led to greater openness in discussions about sex, publicly as well as privately, the pill was central to those conversations. Today that trend continues.

For some young women, the pill has become a central part of their daily routine and a source of bonding with their female friends, even if their relationships with men do not last. Twenty-three-year-old Lauren C reported, "The pill and I are still together, though my high school boyfriend and I are not. . . . My best friend [and I] had been taking it for months already, and we dutifully popped our BB-size tablets at 10 every night. Sometimes it amazes me that I've been taking a drug every day for over five years. That's 1,680 pills, sixty trips to the pharmacy, twenty phone calls to my doctor for refills, and—happily—no pregnancies."[42] Renae J echoed that theme: "While the relationship that brought the pill into my life ended nearly two years ago, my partnership with the pill is stronger than ever. Every morning, the alarm on my cell phone goes off at 10:03, and I reach for the little turquoise packet on my nightstand."[43]

The loyalty to the pill these women express sometimes reflects their lack of trust in men. Lucy T explained, "I am super responsible about sex. Within a month of when I started having sex I was on the pill. . . . I am always prepared. I sometimes even carry a condom in my purse. You can't rely on guys."[44] Regina H agreed that women often use the pill because they "can't trust the men in their lives: to respect their sexual and reproductive choices; to take part in the process of family planning; to support women and their children emotionally, materially, and otherwise."[45]

Yet some men are willing to share the responsibility, improving relationships with their partners. Marianne B felt closer to her partner because of his participation: "I loved that he was willing to pay for half of the expense of the pills (since he was benefiting also) and knew what time I took them and would help remind me when we were on vacation and I was out of my regular routine."[46] Lorena A found that the pill opened discussion "about honesty and health, and about the importance of communication. It also forced us to have 'the talk' about abortion, what we would do if I were to get pregnant. . . . It also opened the door to many a sexual history talk, which is extremely important."[47]

While some women noted improved relationships with male partners who took an interest and shared responsibility for birth control, many more described discussions with their female friends. These discussions not only served as a form of mutual education and information sharing, they also deepened female friendships. Lynn E, a thirty-four-year-old librarian married to her first boyfriend and only sex partner, explained, "I have definitely talked about contraception with friends and my sisters from time to time. . . . I guess these sorts of fairly personal conversations are good for relationships since it brings you a little closer."[48]

Cassie K works for Planned Parenthood, "so of course I discuss contraception often with my work friends and other, mostly female, friends as well. I've found that it's a way of bonding and feel that it's very positive to discuss these things in a way that is unembarrassed."[49] Shelley H agreed: "I have discussed contraception methods with close friends in the past. . . . I guess I feel that it makes relationships closer."[50] If the pill was a bonding experience for some women, not taking the pill could be alienating for others. Alissa S, twenty-eight years old and married for six years, complained, "I feel like a 'freak' because I'm the only woman I know who has never taken the pill. . . . I felt [the pill] was so unnatural, and must truly disrupt our bodies. I am afraid of all the weird side effects. . . . I do feel really left out when the conversation comes around to this topic, though. . . . My girlfriends talk about their experiences trying different brands of birth control pills . . . and I kind of just zone out. When I tell other women I've never taken the pill they kind of act like I'm from another planet. . . . The choice not to take the pill can be isolating in some situations. But I'm OK with that. I think my ovaries are OK with it too."[51]

Sue G was another woman who was unwilling to use artificial forms of contraception. "Cutting off one of my body's normal, natural functions just does not set well with me."[52] Mandy B "barely felt like a woman" while taking the pill, but after she stopped "I could feel the egg release each month and the comforting feeling of my uterine walls shedding as well. I felt like a woman again. I felt like my body was doing what it was supposed to be doing again.[53] Kendra H explained, "There are already so many hormones implanted in our meat and dairy products. Now, when a girl starts having sex, she starts taking the pill, or when a young teenage girl gets a cyst or has a problem getting her period normally—she is automatically prescribed the pill, which is a hormone—a strong hormone—that changes the shape and the function of your body." After she stopped taking the pill, "I feel more confident in knowing that I'm not subjecting my body to hormonal changes that are unnatural." Although she is glad to be off the pill, she has not yet found a satisfactory alternative. "I still hate condoms—they're sticky, gross, smell funny and EVERY GUY has a problem with them. It's annoying that it always falls on the girl to provide some sort of intervention when it comes to this."[54]

One approach that is increasing in popularity with young women who want a natural form of birth control is the Fertility Awareness Method (FAM). Jacqueline G is a FAM enthusiast. She initially took the pill at the age of twenty-six after an unintended pregnancy and abortion. "For the next two and a half years, my body felt numb, my sexuality dimmed, and my brain felt cloudy and dull." Then she heard about FAM. Unlike the rhythm method, which is unreliable because it is based on averages, FAM charts the individual woman's cycle. "I was stunned to hear about scientific birth control that was completely natural and engaged both partners in the method. . . . I told my husband about the method as soon as I got home, and he was as excited about it as I was. (He was disconcerted by my feelings of separation from my own sexuality.) We both loved how natural the method is." Together they took an eight-hour course that "pretty much blew our minds. . . . It was a wild experience, to be able to discuss human sexuality openly with other adults, and to be able to ask the 'stupid' questions that most of us shared." They learned how to chart temperatures and analyze cervical secretions to determine scientifically the exact times she was fertile. "Suddenly my fertility wasn't something wild or uncontrollable, which is how I'd felt after the pregnancy and abortion. . . . It's true that it requires more active participation than the pill or condoms alone, but I find it deeply satisfying to be so attuned to my body's rhythms and fertility signals." Now that both she and her husband know when she is fertile, "It erases the dynamic of 'woman as all-knowing gatekeeper' and 'man as ignorant beggar' when it comes to sex and pregnancy avoidance. It's like we both learned a new language—the language of my body's rhythms." Now, when she sees her doctor, she feels "more empowered to advocate for my health. I now feel like I know as much if not more about my body than my doctors. My health is in my hands."[55]

Jacqueline G's rejection of artificial forms of contraception represents the culmination of the women's health movement and the altered relationship between women and the medical establishment that began when the pill first came on the market in the 1960s. Today's women are more knowledgeable consumers of contraceptive products, but they do not always have the options they would like. Many expressed frustration at doctors, clinics, and nurses who pushed the pill on them when they wanted other alternatives. Unlike their mothers, who may have had difficulty getting access to the pill if they were not married, many single women complained that they are prescribed the pill regardless of their preferences for other forms of contraception. Rebecca H experienced side effects from the pill, but when she requested an IUD from a local clinic she was told it was not appropriate for women who had not had children. "So I left [the clinic] feeling demoralized, dejected, and without any options. They practically threw a new prescription for pills at me."[56]

Anita B was even more perplexed that she was offered a prescription for the pill, since she is not at risk of getting pregnant. As she explained, "I am a femme who partners with fe-male-bodied, masculine-identified partners (butch women and transgender men), although I have had sexual relationships with biological males in the past. My current partner is fe-male. . . . Despite the fact that I have partnered exclusively with female-bodied partners for the past four years, health care providers have repeatedly offered to prescribe the pill for me. They often ask what form of birth control I am using, and sug-gest the pill, AFTER I have told them that my partner is fe-male." She notes that women who appear masculine face the opposite problem. "My butch partners have never been offered the pill; in fact, some of them have been discouraged from seeking routine gynecological care (told that they don't need it). . . . It is also a reminder that my feminine appearance makes my sexual orientation suspect. Health care providers want to prescribe the pill because I LOOK like someone who could—and should—have a male sexual partner. I am young, feminine, fit, and perceived to be fertile, and the medical establishment is eager to regulate my fertility. They have no interest in the fer-tility of my partners, who have all the same female 'parts' but are often mistaken for men on the street."[57]

While some complained about health professionals foisting the pill on women who do not want or need it, others ex-pressed outrage at measures that allow health care providers and pharmacists to refuse treatments and products if they have religious or ethical objections. These "conscience clauses" came into effect in the 1970s after *Roe v. Wade* to allow doctors to refuse to perform abortions if they are morally opposed to it. In 2008, George W. Bush expanded the "conscience clause" provision to allow pharmacists to refuse to fill prescriptions for birth control pills or emergency contraception. Just after taking office, President Obama reversed the Bush expansion.[58]

The women who responded to the Internet survey overwhelmingly and vehemently asserted their demand that the pill, and all other contraceptive options, be available, accessible, and affordable to all. Katie M fumed, "I'm completely pissed off and freaked out that there's been a growing trend of misogyny and 'conscience clauses' that allow pharmacists to refuse to fill legal birth control prescriptions."[59] Krista A insisted, "It's not the pharmacists', priests', pastors', protesters', or anyone else's business what I take ANY medication for."[60]

Amy K was astonished to discover that her doctor would no longer prescribe contraceptives. "To me, birth control has always been a good and safe option. I have never thought it to be immoral or unethical, and it has always been presented to me as a good thing. I never realized how strong my opinions actually were until a few years ago I received a letter from my family doctor saying that he is refusing to prescribe birth control to his patients and would use natural family planning instead. I was livid. . . . Who was he to limit the choices of his patients?"[61]

Others encountered more subtle roadblocks to access, particularly for the morning-after pill. This pill is a form of emergency contraception that can be taken after unprotected sex. Since the 1970s, doctors and their patients have known that an increased dose of oral contraceptives taken after intercourse can prevent an egg from being fertilized. In the late 1990s, the FDA approved two morning-after pill compounds, Plan B and

Preven, for use as emergency contraception with a doctor's prescription. Since 2004, the American Academy of Pediatrics and the Society of Adolescent Medicine have urged the FDA to allow women and girls as young as fourteen access to the morning-after pill without a prescription. But the proposal faced opposition from religious conservatives, abortion foes, and the Bush administration. Efforts to make the morning-after pill available over the counter were thwarted until 2006, when the FDA approved sale of the drug to women eighteen or older. In 2009, seventeen-year-olds gained access to over-the-counter emergency contraception.[62]

The issue of access and availability is all the more pressing for the morning-after pill, when time is of the essence and the stakes are high. Krista A noted, "Morning-after pills are a great way to make sure a single night of passion doesn't ruin a woman's life."[63] But emergency contraception can still be difficult to obtain, even for those who are legally eligible to buy it without a prescription. Cathy P recounted a frustrating effort to secure the morning-after pill. "They claim it's sold 'over the counter,' but I still had to go stand in line at the pharmacists counter just to ask for permission to buy it. I wouldn't have minded doing that, but I had to go to six different pharmacies . . . before finding one that had emergency contraception in stock. . . . I understood when I was told the first time, 'Sorry, we're out of stock.' But five times?! Maybe there was a freakish epidemic of careless sex and coincidental condom breakage the night before . . . but I have my doubts." When she finally found a pharmacy where she was able to obtain it, she was humiliated when "a random guy did some lame little catcall in passing. Ugh. I had the overwhelming urge to just turn around and lash out at him while waving that box of Plan B in his face like a crazed lunatic. But I just kept walking."[64]

These stories and commentaries of encounters with the pill illuminate the many ways women's lives have changed. More than simply an effective means of birth control, the oral contraceptive has played a central role in women's sexuality, relationships, political beliefs, and identity. Whether they love the pill or hate it, whether they faced parental opposition or support, whether single or married, whether religious or not, their testimonies reflect the profound ways in which the pill has become embedded in both public and private life.

Conclusion

When the history of the 20th century is written,
it may be seen as the first when men and women
were truly partners. Wonderful things can come in
small packets.

The Economist, naming the birth
control pill one of the Seven Wonders
of the Modern World, 1993.[1]

After fifty years on the market, has the pill fulfilled the
utopian dreams it inspired in 1960? The answer is yes and
no. The pill did not solve what many at the time saw as the
most pressing problem facing the world: the population explosion. Nor did it put an end to war or poverty. It did not eradicate unhappy marriages, unwanted pregnancies, abortions, or
unwed motherhood. It was not the magic pill that would prevent pregnancy with no side effects or health risks. It did not
unleash a sexual revolution or alter the sexual habits of the unmarried. The pill was not the pharmacological engine for any

mega-transformations in our social, cultural, or personal lives. It was, however, central to some of the most profound developments in both public and private life over the last half century.

Although the pill was not responsible for the emancipation of women, it did provide an important tool for millions of women to effectively control their fertility, freeing them from fears of pregnancy and constant childbearing and enabling them to take advantage of expanding opportunities for education, employment, and participation in public life. The feminist movement made it possible for women to use the pill to improve their lives and to use their collective power to improve the pill as well.

Today's pill has little in common with its 1960 original. Containing only a small fraction of the amount of hormones in the original dose, it is "not your mother's birth control pill," as the *New York Times* noted. The new formulas reflect improvements resulting from half a century of extensive research and more studies of its safety than any pharmaceutical product in history. A 1999 study reporting on twenty-five years of follow-up with more than 45,000 women demonstrated that the oral contraceptive pill is safe and effective.[2]

Contraceptive use has also changed. Today, 98 percent of all women who have ever had heterosexual intercourse have used some form of contraception; 82 percent have used oral contraceptives. The pill remains the leading method of birth control in the United States. Since 1982 the pill and female sterilization have been the two most widely used forms of contraception. The percentage of women who used birth control at their first sexual encounter has also increased dramatically, from

43 percent in the 1970s to 79 percent today; although the method was most often condoms, the use of the pill also increased.[3]

For all its improvements and its widespread use, the pill is still not the ideal contraceptive. Some risks and side effects remain. Although it offers excellent protection against pregnancy when taken properly, the pill is less reliable than other methods, especially the IUD, the patch, and the implant, which have lower failure rates because they do not require that the woman remember to take a pill every day. But pregnancy is no longer the most dreaded outcome of unprotected sex, especially now that both abortion and emergency contraception are legal. More frightening and more dangerous are sexually transmitted diseases (STDs), especially HIV/AIDS. Hormonal contraceptives provide no protection against STDs, which can be incurable and even deadly. As one young woman lamented, "I think there was probably the perception once upon a time that the birth control pill took away the consequences of sex, but HIV/AIDS has been around for my entire life."[4] For that reason, many women prefer to use barrier methods that protect against STDs, sometimes in addition to taking the pill.[5] The oral contraceptive is among a cornucopia of contraceptive products available—IUDs, patches, implants, rings, drugs that reduce the number of menstrual cycles or eliminate them altogether—yet none of them is perfect. There is still a demand for better contraceptives that offer protection against both pregnancy and STDs, without risks or side effects.

The story of the pill is not over. Although hormonal contraceptives are now widely available in many forms, obstacles of cost and availability still make it difficult for some women to get it when they need it. Access is still compromised by laws and policies that shift with the political winds. Yet it is clear that the birth control pill has come of age. It is safe and effective for most women. Its developers and marketers listened to women who demanded safer contraceptives, easier access, more information, and further research. The feminist movement not only empowered women to make demands on the medical and pharmaceutical establishments, it also opened the doors for women to join men in these previously male-dominated enterprises. As increasing numbers of women entered the fields of science and medicine, the developers and providers of contraceptive products were also likely to be the consumers of those products.[6]

From beginning to end, women were largely responsible for the pill's success. The oral contraceptive was promoted and developed because of the passion, commitment, and energy of Margaret Sanger and Katharine McCormick. Hundreds of women volunteered for risky clinical trials to help bring it to market, and then millions of women quickly made it the most popular form of birth control in the country and one of the best-selling drugs in U.S. history.[7]

The pill contributed to the empowerment of women not only by allowing them to control their fertility, but also by changing the relationships between women and their doctors and by mobilizing women to take on large pharmaceutical companies, the Catholic Church, and the government. In their personal lives, women found that the pill opened up conversations and contributed to increased intimacy not only with their male partners but with their female friends and relatives. For many women, the process of deciding whether or not to take the pill led them to greater awareness of their bodies, their sexuality, and their reproductive choices. Some women found their way to feminism through their experiences with the pill. Others discovered the extent to which their personal values reflected or diverged from those of their peers and parents.

Without the political and cultural upheavals of the last fifty years, particularly those brought about by the feminist movement, the pill would have been just one more contraceptive—more effective and convenient than those that came before, but not revolutionary. Instead, it became a flash point for major social transformation. The pill played a key role in the movement for reproductive rights, the achievement of standards of informed consent in medical research, and the requirement that pharmaceutical companies provide consumers with information about risks and side effects. It served to highlight the need for new male contraceptives. It was at the center of policy debates over foreign aid and family planning. It ignited skirmishes in the culture wars. Most important, women used it as a powerful tool not only to control their fertility, but to change their lives.

ACKNOWLEDGMENTS

I would like to thank several people for their help with this project. Courtney Martin provided invaluable advice and assistance with the Internet survey and helped to organize and interpret the responses. Jeff Manuel, Matthew Schneider-Meyerson, and Jason Stahl provided outstanding research assistance. I am extremely grateful to Sara Evans, Susan Faludi, Lary May, and Riv-Ellen Prell, who read the entire manuscript and gave me thoughtful comments and suggestions. Thanks also to all those at Basic Books who helped with the production, including Whitney Casser, Susanne Caulfield, Laura Esterman, Lara Heimert, and Amanda Moon, and to Elizabeth Bell for her excellent copyediting. My agent, Sandra Dijkstra, was a wonderful shepherd for the book from beginning to end.

NOTES

INTRODUCTION

1. John Rock, quoted in Lara Marks, *Sexual Chemistry: A History of the Contraceptive Pill* (New Haven, CT: Yale University Press, 2001), p. 13.

2. Elizabeth Siegel Watkins, *On the Pill: A Social History of Oral Contraceptives, 1950–1970* (Baltimore: Johns Hopkins University Press, 1998), pp. 39–40.

3. Andrea Tone, *Devices and Desires: A History of Contraceptives in America* (New York: Hill and Wang, 2001), pp. 203, 227–228, 233–236. There is no data available on the number of unmarried women who took the pill in its first decade on the market. See Chapter 4 in this book.

4. Throughout the book, respondents to the Internet survey are identified by first name and last initial. In the endnotes I have included any information about the respondents that they provided, such as age, religion, occupation, marital status, sexual orientation, and racial or ethnic background.

5. For this revelation I am indebted to Margaret Marsh and Wanda Ronner, whose outstanding biography of John Rock contains the story. See Margaret Marsh and Wanda Ronner, *The Fertility Doctor: John Rock and the Reproductive Revolution* (Baltimore: Johns Hopkins University Press, 2008), pp. 215–221. The detailed account of the FDA approval process is in Suzanne White Junod and Lara

Marks, "Women's Trials: The Approval of the First Oral Contraceptive Pill in the United States and Great Britain," *Journal of the History of Medicine*, vol. 57 (April 2002), pp. 117–160. I have drawn on these works to recount the story at the end of Chapter 1 in this book.

CHAPTER 1

1. "(Since I've Got) The Pill," writers Don McHan, Loretta Lynn, T. D. Bayless, © Copyright 1973, Renewed 2001. Guaranty Music/BMI/Coal Miners Music, Inc./BMI (admin. By EverGreen Copyrights). All rights reserved. Used by permission.

2. For an excellent history of abortion before 1973, see Leslie J. Reagan, *When Abortion Was a Crime* (Berkeley: University of California Press, 1997). See also James Reed, *The Birth Control Movement and American Society: From Private Vice to Public Virtue* (Princeton, NJ: Princeton University Press, 1984).

3. Elaine Tyler May, *Barren in the Promised Land: Childless Americans and the Pursuit of Happiness* (New York: Basic Books, 1995), pp. 46–54.

4. Linda Gordon, *The Moral Property of Women: A History of Birth Control Politics in America* (Urbana: University of Illinois Press, 2002 edition). Quote on page 34. For an outstanding discussion of this history, see John D'Emilio and Estelle B. Freedman, *Intimate Matters: A History of Sexuality in America* (Chicago: University of Chicago Press, 1988, 1997), especially Parts II and III.

5. Gordon, *Moral Property*, p. 138.

6. Quoted in Gordon, *Moral Property*, p. 150; see also p. 157.

7. See Gordon, *Moral Property*, Chapter 8.

8. Lara V. Marks, *Sexual Chemistry: A History of the Contraceptive Pill* (New Haven, CT: Yale University Press, 2001), pp. 51–52.

9. Gordon, *Moral Property*, p. 157.

10. No byline, "Disorder in Court as Sanger Is Fined," *New York Times*, September 11, 1915, unpaginated pdf file, New York Times online, accessed 8/11/08.

11. Quoted in Gordon, *Moral Property*, p. 221.

12. See Gordon, *Moral Property*, Chapter 11.

13. Quoted in Andrea Tone, *Devices and Desires: A History of Contraceptives in America* (New York: Hill and Wang, 2001), p. 207; and Bernard Asbell, *The Pill: A Biography of the Drug that Changed the World* (New York: Random House, 1995), p. 9.

14. Tone, *Devices and Desires*, pp. 204–205.

15. Marks, *Sexual Chemistry*, pp. 53–54.

16. Quoted in Tone, *Devices and Desires*, p. 214; and Asbell, *The Pill*, p. 234.

17. Elizabeth Siegel Watkins, *On the Pill: A Social History of Oral Contraceptives, 1950–1970* (Baltimore: Johns Hopkins University Press, 1998), pp. 25–26.

18. Sheldon J. Segal, *Under the Banyan Tree* (New York: Oxford University Press, 2003), p. 71.

19. Tone, *Devices and Desires*, pp. 209–214.

20. There are several excellent accounts of the development of the pill. These include Marks, *Sexual Chemistry*; Tone, *Devices and Desires*; Asbell, *The Pill*, Book 1; Watkins, *On the Pill*, Chapter 1; and the PBS documentary *The Pill*, produced for the *American Experience*, along with its Web site www.pbs.org/wgbh/amex/pill/filmmore/index.html.

21. Sanger and Pincus quoted in Marks, *Sexual Chemistry*, p. 37.

22. Carl Djerassi, *This Man's Pill* (New York: Oxford University Press, 2001).

23. The author remembers her father, Edward T. Tyler, M.D., giving this explanation many times when asked about his research on both infertility and contraception.

24. Margaret Marsh and Wanda Ronner, *The Fertility Doctor: John Rock and the Reproductive Revolution* (Baltimore: Johns Hopkins University Press, 2008), Chapter 1.

25. Quoted in Tone, *Devices and Desires*, p. 217. For an in-depth account of John Rock's life, work, research, and Catholicism, see Marsh and Ronner, *The Fertility Doctor*; Loretta McLaughlin, *The*

Pill, John Rock, and the Church: The Biography of a Revolution (Boston: Little, Brown and Co., 1982); and John Rock, *The Time Has Come: A Catholic Doctor's Proposals to End the Battle Over Birth Control* (New York: Alfred A. Knopf, 1963).

26. See Marsh and Ronner, *The Fertility Doctor.*

27. Tone, *Devices and Desires*, pp. 216–219, quote is on p. 219.

28. Tone, *Devices and Desires*, pp. 219–220.

29. Marks, *Sexual Chemistry,* Chapter 4. The discussion of the clinical trials here is largely drawn from Marks's study.

30. Quoted in Marks, *Sexual Chemistry*, p. 98.

31. Tone, *Devices and Desires*, pp. 220–221. See also Chapter 9 for an excellent discussion of the development of the pill.

32. Quotes are from Tone, *Devices and Desires*, p. 223–224.

33. Tone, *Devices and Desires,* pp. 223–224.

34. Marks, *Sexual Chemistry*, p. 114.

35. Suzanne White Junod and Lara Marks, "Women's Trials: The Approval of the First Oral Contraceptive Pill in the United States and Great Britain," *Journal of the History of Medicine*, vol. 57 (April 2002), pp. 117–160.

36. Quoted in Junod and Marks, "Women's Trials," p. 130, footnote 33.

37. Tone, *Devices and Desires*, p. 231; for a detailed study of the approval process of the pill, and Edward Tyler's role in it, see Junod and Marks, "Women's Trials," especially pp. 131–133; see also Marsh and Ronner, *The Fertility Doctor*, pp. 219–221.

CHAPTER 2

1. Hugh Moore, quoted in Lara V. Marks, *Sexual Chemistry: A History of the Contraceptive Pill* (New Haven, CT: Yale University Press, 2001), p. 28.

2. The author attended this conference and remembers it vividly. After the presentation, during informal conversations, many of the

Indian physicians predicted that the pill would not work in India. It turned out that they were correct.

3. See Marks, *Sexual Chemistry*, especially Chapter 1. Some researchers were dubious about claims that the pill would prove to be a panacea for overpopulation, including John Rock, who believed that the pill would be of little value in places like India, especially in rural areas where women had no access to education, no rights, and no privacy. See Margaret Marsh and Wanda Ronner, *The Fertility Doctor: John Rock and the Reproductive Revolution* (Baltimore: Johns Hopkins University Press, 2008), pp. 200–201.

4. Quoted in Linda Gordon, *The Moral Property of Women: A History of Birth Control Politics in America* (Urbana: University of Illinois Press, 2002 edition), p. 147.

5. See Matthew Connelly, *Fatal Misconception: The Struggle to Control World Population* (Cambridge, MA: Harvard University Press, 2008), for a powerful critique of the population control movement. He notes the distinction between the two terms on p. 16.

6. James Reed, *From Private Vice to Public Virtue: The Birth Control Movement and American Society Since 1830* (New York: Basic Books, 1978), pp. 102, 144, and 187.

7. Abraham Stone, "The Control of Fertility," *Scientific American*, April 1954, p. 31; on Sanger's opposition see Ellen Chesler, *Woman of Valor: Margaret Sanger and the Birth Control Movement in America* (New York: Simon and Schuster, 1992), pp. 393–394.

8. Marks, *Sexual Chemistry*, pp. 21–22; Elaine Tyler May, *Homeward Bound: American Families in the Cold War Era* (New York: Basic Books, 2008 edition), pp. 142–143.

9. See Elizabeth Siegel Watkins, *On the Pill: A Social History of Oral Contraceptives, 1950–1970* (Baltimore: Johns Hopkins University Press, 1998), pp. 16–19; Sheldon J. Segal, *Under the Banyan Tree* (New York: Oxford University Press, 2003), p. xviii.

10. Marks, *Sexual Chemistry*, pp. 31–34.

11. Quoted in Gordon, *Moral Property of Women*, p. 284.

12. Quoted in Marks, *Sexual Chemistry*, p. 28.

13. *U.S. News & World Report* articles: "Surging Population: An 'Erupting Volcano,' " 52, 20 (May 14, 1962), p. 9; "An Overcrowded World?" 45, 9 (Aug. 29, 1958), p. 48; "Too Many People in the World?" 41, 2 (July 13, 1956), p. 80; "As Population Keeps Climbing," 46, 1 (Jan. 2, 1959), p. 54; "Asia's 'Boom' in Babies," 51, 6 (August 7, 1961), p. 66; "World Choice: Limit Population or Face Famine," 58, 24 (June 14, 1965), p. 64; and "The World's Biggest Problem," 55, 13 (Sept. 16, 1963), p. 60; "Where Will U.S. Put 60 Million More People?" 43, 6 (Aug. 9, 1957), p. 46; "How the Population Boom Will Change America," 45, 22 (Nov. 28, 1958), p. 86; "Breakthrough in Birth Control: Answer to Population Explosion?" 59, 14 (Oct. 4, 1965), p. 56. David Lyle, "The Human Race Has, Maybe, Thirty-Five Years Left," *Esquire* LXVII, 3 (Whole No. 406) (September 1967), p. 116.

14. Marks, *Sexual Chemistry*, pp. 29–31.

15. Quoted in Tone, *Devices and Desires*, p. 214; and Asbell, *The Pill*, p. 234.

16. Edward G. Stockwell, *Population and People* (Chicago: Quadrangle Books, 1968), pp. 5–11; See also Margaret O. Hyde, *This Crowded Planet* (New York: McGraw-Hill, 1961).

17. Paul Ehrlich quoted in Connelly, *Fatal Misconception*, p. 259; Asbell, *The Pill*, pp. 326–328.

18. Connelly, *Fatal Misconception*, pp. 239, 259.

19. No byline, *Life*, April 17, 1970, vol. 68, no. 14.

20. Gordon Rattray Taylor, chief science adviser to the British Broadcasting Company, "People Pollution . . . " *Ladies Home Journal*, October 1970, pp. 74–80; Leyhausen quoted on p. 78.

21. No byline, "Our Multiplying Families," *Changing Times*, The Kiplinger Magazine, May 1966, p. 6.

22. David Lyle, "The Human Race Has, Maybe, Thirty-Five Years Left," *Esquire* LXVII, 3 (Whole No. 406) (September 1967), pp. 182–183.

23. See Elaine Tyler May, *Barren in the Promised Land: Childless Americans and the Pursuit of Happiness* (New York: Basic Books, 1995), pp. 114–119.

24. Johanna Schoen, *Choice and Coercion: Birth Control, Sterilization, and Abortion in Public Health and Welfare* (Chapel Hill: University of North Carolina Press, 2005), pp. 2–3.

25. Schoen, *Choice and Coercion*, pp. 4–12.

26. "How to Plan a Family," *Ebony* magazine, July 1948, pp. 13–15, quoted in "Case for Birth Control," *Newsweek*, 31 January 1955, pp. 60–61.

27. See, for example, Gordon, *Moral Property of Women*, p. 200; Marks, *Sexual Chemistry*, p. 20.

28. Quoted in Dorothy Roberts, *Killing the Black Body: Race, Reproduction, and the Meaning of Liberty* (New York: Pantheon, 1997), pp. 76–77.

29. Legal scholar Dorothy Roberts concluded that Sanger was motivated by a genuine desire to improve the lives of the poor women she served. See Roberts, *Killing the Black Body*, quotes on p. 81.

30. In the same year, he abandoned his former name, LeRoi Jones, to become Amiri Baraka.

31. Discussion of Black Power leaders' opposition and quote from Dawes in Roberts, *Killing the Black Body*, pp. 98–99, quote on p. 99.

32. Quotes are from Roberts, *Killing the Black Body*, p. 100. Emphasis in the original.

33. Roberts, *Killing the Black Body*, pp. 100–101, quotes on p. 100; Ralph Z. Hallow, "The Blacks Cry Genocide," *The Nation*, April 28, 1969, pp. 535–537.

34. Legal scholar Dorothy Roberts noted, "We must acknowledge the justice of ensuring equal access to birth control for poor and minority women without denying the injustice of imposing birth control as a means of reducing their fertility." See Roberts, *Killing the Black Body*, pp. 56–57; Ralph Z. Hallow, "The Blacks Cry Genocide," *The Nation*, April 28, 1969, p. 537.

35. Asbell, *The Pill,* pp. 326–328.
36. Segal, *Under the Banyan Tree,* p. xxvii.
37. Ibid., p. xviii.
38. For data supporting these claims, see Connelly, *Fatal Misconception,* pp. 374–376.
39. Segal, *Under the Banyan Tree,* p. xv.
40. Asbell, *The Pill,* pp. 326–328; Segal, *Under the Banyan Tree,* p. xii.
41. Segal, *Under the Banyan Tree,* p. xxviii.
42. Ibid., pp. xxiv, xxviii.
43. Connelly, *Fatal Misconception,* p. 373.

CHAPTER 3

1. Both quotes are from Robert W. Kistner, M.D., "What 'The Pill' Does to Husbands," *Ladies Home Journal,* January 1969, pp. 66, 68.
2. See Elaine Tyler May, *Homeward Bound: American Families in the Cold War Era* (New York: Basic Books, 2008).
3. Joyce Johnson, *Minor Characters: A Beat Memoir* (New York: Penguin, 1999).
4. "The Pill Versus The Springhill Mine Disaster" from *The Pill Versus The Springhill Mine Disaster,* by Richard Brautigan. Copyright © by Richard Brautigan. Reprinted by permission of Houghton Mifflin Harcourt Publishing Company. All rights reserved.
5. Elizabeth Fraterrigo, *Playboy and the Making of the Good Life in Modern America* (New York: Oxford University Press, 2009), readership on p. 1.
6. See Barbara Ehrenreich, *The Hearts of Men: American Dreams and the Flight from Commitment* (New York: Anchor Books/Doubleday, 1983).
7. Carrie Pitzulo, "The Battle in Every Man's Bed: *Playboy* and the Fiery Feminists," *Journal of the History of Sexuality* 17, 2 (May 2008), pp. 259–289. On funding for Masters and Johnson, see Thomas Maier, *Masters of Sex: The Life and Times of William Masters and Vir-*

ginia Johnson, the Couple Who Taught America How to Love (New York: Basic Books, 2009), pp. 203–206.

8. Philip Wylie, "The Womanization of America," *Playboy*, September 1958; a forum including comments by Edward Bernays, Dr. Ernest Dichter, Alexander King, Norman Mailer, Herbert Mayes, Dr. Ashley Montagu, Dr. Theodor Reik, and Mort Sahl, "The Playboy Panel: The Womanization of America," *Playboy*, June 1962, vol. 9, issue 6, pp. 43 et seq.

9. Ibid.

10. Quotes are from the Playboy Panel, June 1962, p. 46.

11. Cartoons are from *Playboy*, April 1960, vol. 7, issue 4; January 1961, vol. 8, issue 1; January 1962, vol. 9, issue 1.

12. *Playboy*, 1964, vol. 11, issue 5, p. 170; *Playboy*, 1964, vol. 11, issue 5, p. 145.

13. *Playboy*, 1965, vol. 12, issue 7; p. 202; 1965, vol. 12, issue 4, p. 161.

14. *Playboy*, 1965 vol. 12, issue 9, p. 258; 1966, vol.13, issue 7, p. 100.

15. Hugh M. Hefner, "The Playboy Philosophy," *Playboy*, January 1964, vol. 11, issue 1, p. 64; responses in *Playboy*, May 1964, vol. 11, issue 5, p. 55

16. "(Name Withheld by request)," Grenada Hills, California, "Playboy Forum," and Stephen L. Larson, M.D., Rochester, Minnesota, "Alternative to Abortion," in *Playboy*, 1966, vol. 13, issue 5, p. 135; Harry Clark, Cleveland, Ohio, "Abortion: Doctors' View"; Mark Ross, University of California, Santa Barbara, "Contraception and Abortion"; Kenneth Sherwood, Lehigh University, Bethlehem, Pennsylvania, "Birth-Control Ban"; and Thomas Gibbons, Los Angeles, California, "Catholics and the Pill," all in the "Playboy Forum" of *Playboy*, 1967, vol. 14, issue 8, p. 37.

17. Hugh Hefner, "The Playboy Philosophy," *Playboy*, 1964, vol. 11, issue 7, p. 115.

18. By the mid-1960s female readers began to write to the magazine. It is not altogether certain that female writers actually wrote all

the letters attributed to women. Some letters with the "name withheld" may have been generated by the editors in order for *Playboy* to argue against the views expressed. Either way, *Playboy* was not sympathetic to women who were reluctant to take the pill.

19. Charleen Dimmick, New Orleans, Louisiana, "Perils of the Pill," and response by the editors, *Playboy*, 1967, vol. 13, issue 1, pp. 63–64.

20. "(Name Withheld by Request)," Letter to the Editor, and Editor's Reply, "Perils of the Pill," *Playboy*, 1967, vol. 14, issue 11, p. 164. Response quoted a study by Dr. Frederick J. Ziegler of the Cleveland Clinic Foundation.

21. "The Pill," *Redbook*, January 1966, p. 76, quoted in Tone, *Devices and Desires*, p. 252.

22. Quoted in Linda Witt, "The Male Contraceptive, A Bitter Pill?" *Today's Health*, June 1970, p. 18.

23. Quoted in Witt, "Male Contraceptive," p. 18.

24. Kistner was widely regarded as one of the leading experts on oral contraceptives. He also served as an expert witness for Searle in a suit resulting from the death of a woman from thromboembolic disease in 1965. See Margaret Marsh and Wanda Ronner, *The Fertility Doctor: John Rock and the Reproductive Revolution* (Baltimore: Johns Hopkins University Press, 2008), pp. 260, 262.

25. All of these quotes are from experts quoted in Robert W. Kistner, M.D., "What 'The Pill' Does to Husbands," *Ladies Home Journal*, January 1969, pp. 66, 68.

26. Quotes are from Kistner, "What 'The Pill' Does to Husbands."

27. Kistner and other experts are quoted in Kistner, "What 'The Pill' Does to Husbands."

CHAPTER 4

1. Gloria Steinem, "The Moral Disarmament of Betty Coed," *Esquire* LVIII, 3 (Whole no. 346) September 1962, pp. 97, 153–157, quote on p. 155.

2. Pearl S. Buck, in *Readers Digest*, quoted in Elizabeth Siegel Watkins, *On the Pill: A Social History of Oral Contraceptives, 1950–1970* (Baltimore: Johns Hopkins University Press, 1998) p. 66.

3. Beth Bailey, *Sex in the Heartland* (Cambridge, MA: Harvard University Press, 1999), p. 106.

4. Quotes are from Steinem, "Moral Disarmament," p. 153.

5. See John D'Emilio and Estelle B. Freedman, *Intimate Matters: A History of Sexuality in America* (Chicago: University of Chicago Press, 1988, 1997), especially Chapter 13.

6. Dr. John Gagnon and clinical psychologist Isadore Rubin quoted in Bernard Asbell, *The Pill: A Biography of the Drug that Changed the World* (New York: Random House, 1995), p. 198.

7. Steinem, "Moral Disarmament," pp. 155–157.

8. Stephanie Coontz, *The Way We Never Were: American Families and the Nostalgia Trap* (New York: Basic Books, 2000 edition), pp. 182–183, 194, 202; Watkins, *On the Pill*, p. 9.

9. Coontz, *The Way We Never Were*, pp. 194, 198; D'Emilio and Freedman, *Intimate Matters*, p. 286; Asbell, *The Pill*, p. 200.

10. D'Emilio and Freedman, *Intimate Matters*, Chapters 10 and 11.

11. Quoted in Linda Gordon, *The Moral Property of Women: A History of Birth Control Politics in America* (Urbana: University of Illinois Press, 2002 edition), pp. 151–152.

12. D'Emilio and Freedman, *Intimate Matters*, Part II. These views were also reflected in early motion pictures. Seven films between 1916 and 1939 dealt with birth control, taking on the controversies. Each film was explicitly either for or against contraception. Those that promoted birth control, including Margaret Sanger's documentary *Birth Control* (1917) and the feature film *The Hand that Rocks the Cradle* (1917), show the dangers to women of having too many children and the folly of making birth control illegal. Those that opposed contraception, such as *Where Are My Children?* (1916) and *The House Without Children* (1919), condemned the "modern" woman who tried to prevent pregnancy as immoral and anti-family. In Cecil B. DeMille's

biggest box-office failure, *Four Frightened People* (1934), westerners marooned on an island of "pygmies" try to teach birth control to native women. *Unborn Souls* (1939) promotes birth control as the positive alternative to illegal abortion. After *Unborn Souls* was released, birth control disappeared from American screens until the 1950s, when two films touched very lightly on the subject. *Cheaper by the Dozen* (1950), based on a true story, includes a brief scene when the mother of twelve is approached to be the president of a local Planned Parenthood chapter; *Full of Life* (1957) includes graphic discussions of pregnancy and birth control and was criticized for being in bad taste. Film plots and reviews were gathered at the Herrick Library, Academy of Motion Picture Arts and Sciences, Los Angeles.

13. See Elaine Tyler May, *Homeward Bound: American Families in the Cold War Era* (New York: Basic Books, 2008).

14. See Leslie Reagan, *When Abortion Was a Crime: Women, Medicine, and Law in the United States, 1867–1973* (Berkeley: University of California Press, 1997).

15. See Rickie Solinger, *Wake Up Little Susie: Single Pregnancy and Race before Roe v. Wade* (New York: Routledge, 1992).

16. Mary McCarthy, "Dottie Makes an Honest Woman of Herself," *Partisan Review*, January-February 1954, pp. 34–52. Quotes are from pp. 34 and 52. See also Nancy K. Miller, "Women's Secrets and the Novel: Remembering Mary McCarthy's *The Group*," *Social Research*, Vol. 68, 2001.

17. Philip Roth, *Goodbye, Columbus* (Boston: Houghton Mifflin Co., 1959).

18. Philip Roth interview with Terry Gross, *Fresh Air*, National Public Radio, 2005, rebroadcast April 11, 2008.

19. *Mad Men* season 1, episode 1, "Smoke Gets in Your Eyes," AMC, 2007.

20. Watkins, *On the Pill*, pp. 2, 44–45, 54–55, quote from *Mademoiselle* on pp. 44–45.

21. Bailey, *Sex in the Heartland*, p. 119.

22. Watkins, *On the Pill*, pp. 58–59.

23. Quoted in Watkins, *On the Pill*, pp. 65–66.

24. Asbell, *The Pill*, p. 196.

25. Watkins, *On the Pill*, pp. 66–67; Asbell, *The Pill*, pp. 196, 198; D'Emilio and Freedman, *Intimate Matters*, p. 251.

26. Quoted in Andrea Tone, *Devices and Desires: A History of Contraceptives in America* (New York: Hill and Wang, 2001), p. 236.

27. No byline, "The Second Sexual Revolution," *Time*, January 24, 1964, pp. 54–59, quotes on pp. 55–58.

28. No byline, "No Moral Revolution Discovered, Yet," *Science News*, 93, 3 (Jan. 20, 1968), pp. 60–61.

29. Reiss quoted in Asbell, *The Pill*, pp. 198–199; Ira L. Reiss, *The Social Context of Premarital Sexual Permissiveness* (New York: Holt, Rinehart and Winston, 1967).

30. Sean Goldberg, San Francisco, California, "Morning-After Pill," *Playboy*, 1967, vol. 4, issue 7, p. 133.

31. Watkins, *On the Pill*, pp. 60, 63–64; Asbell, *The Pill*, pp. 200, 206–207; Watkins, *On the Pill*, pp. 58–59.

32. Rebecca L, e-mail response to Internet survey.

33. Eleanor S, e-mail response to Internet survey.

34. Bailey, *Sex in the Heartland*, esp. Chapter 4.

35. Bailey, *Sex in the Heartland*, p. 110; Watkins, *On the Pill*, p. 2.

36. Asbell, *The Pill*, pp. 195, 198.

37. Asbell, *The Pill*, p. 201.

38. Bailey, *Sex in the Heartland*, p. 120.

39. Bailey, *Sex in the Heartland*, pp. 120–130.

40. *Goodbye Columbus* and *Prudence and the Pill*, viewed by the author. Other film plot summaries derived from listings at the Herrick Library, Academy of Motion Picture Arts and Sciences, Los Angeles.

CHAPTER 5

1. Internet survey respondent Leslie C, age 27, 2008.

2. Nelly Oudshoorn, *The Male Pill: A Biography of a Technology in the Making* (Durham, NC: Duke University Press, 2003), pp. 29–31.

3. No byline, "Birth control: Is male contraception the answer?" *Good Housekeeping*, April 1969, vol. 168, no. 4, pp. 201–203, quote on p. 202.

4. Oudshoorn, *The Male Pill*, pp. 6–10, 46.

5. George Gallup, "Male Sterilization Approved," *Boston Globe*, September 4, 1970, unpaginated clipping, clipping file of the Arthur and Elizabeth Schlesinger Library on the History of Women in America, Radcliffe Institute for Advanced Study, Cambridge, MA (hereafter cited as "Schlesinger clipping file").

6. Elizabeth Canfield, editor, *Emko Newsletter*, August 1973, p. 2 (Schlesinger clipping file).

7. Oudshoorn, *The Male Pill*, pp. 24, 70–73, 87–88; Tone, *Devices and Desires: A History of Contraceptives in America* (New York: Hill and Wang, 2001), pp. 253–254.

8. Harold Jackson, "Chemical Methods of Male Contraception," quoted in Oudshoorn, *The Male Pill*, p. 19.

9. Quoted in Oudshoorn, *The Male Pill*, p. 21.

10. Oudshoorn, *The Male Pill*, pp. 39–40, 72.

11. Ibid., pp. 21, 47, quote on p. 47.

12. Quoted in Oudshoorn, *The Male Pill*, p. 19.

13. Quoted in Tone, *Devices and Desires*, p. 253.

14. Letters are quoted in Tone, *Devices and Desires*, pp. 246–247.

15. Dr. Lindsay R. Curtis, "Pill for men? Research under way," *Boston Globe*, November 13, 1970, unpaginated clipping, Schlesinger clipping file.

16. Gregory Pincus, *The Control of Fertility* (New York: Academic Press, 1965), p. 194, quoted in Elizabeth Siegel Watkins, *On the Pill: A Social History of Oral Contraceptives, 1950–1970* (Baltimore: Johns Hopkins University Press, 1998), p. 20.

17. Quoted in Tone, *Devices and Desires*, p. 252.

18. Oudshoorn, *The Male Pill*, pp. 87–110, quote on page 107.

19. Victor Cohn, "Pill scare, lib movement place birth onus on male," *The Washington Post*, undated clipping, 1970, Schlesinger clipping file.

20. Ernest Dunbar, "Foolproof Birth Control," *Look*, March 9, 1971, p. 45, Schlesinger clipping file.

21. Dr. Lindsay R. Curtis, "Male reader asks about sterilization," *Boston Globe*, October 7, 1970, unpaginated clipping, Schlesinger clipping file.

22. John J. Fried, "The Incision Decision," *Esquire* LXXVII, 6 (Whole No. 463) (June 1972), pp. 118–177.

23. Oudshoorn, *The Male Pill*, p. 67; L. Witt, "The Male Contraceptive: A Bitter Pill?" *Today's Health*, June 1970, pp. 17–20, 60–63.

24. Jennifer Macleod, "How to Hold a Wife: A Bridegroom's Guide," *Village Voice*, February 11, 1971, p. 5, quoted in Tone, *Devices and Desires*, p. 251.

25. B. Cowan, "Breakthrough in Male Contraception," *Spare Rib*, April 1980, issue 93, p. 9, reprinted from *East Bay Men's Centre Newsletter* and *The Periodical Lunch*, Ann Arbor, Michigan. Illustration by Dawn Bracey, Schlesinger clipping file.

26. No byline, "Tiny Gold Valves to Control Fertility," *Life*, July 28, 1972, pp. 54–56.

27. Witt, "The Male Contraceptive," p. 20.

28. Victor Cohn, "Contraceptive cream for males proposed," *Boston Globe*, August 20, 1983, unpaginated clipping; Associated Press, "Contraceptive Salve for Men Reported Ready for Testing," unidentified clipping (both in Schlesinger clipping file).

29. Quoted in David M. Rorvik, "What's better than the Pill, Vasectomy, Celibacy and Rhythm?" *Esquire* LXXXII, 1 (Whole No. 494) (January 1975), pp. 100–158.

30. Ibid.

31. No byline, World Book Science Service, "Antifertility Drug Developed for Men, Rats," *Minneapolis Tribune*, July 7, 1970, unpaginated clipping, Schlesinger clipping file. The compound was also

mentioned as a promising male contraceptive in "Birth Control: is male contraception the answer?" in *Good Housekeeping*, April 1969, vol. 168, no. 4, p. 202.

32. Witt, "The Male Contraceptive," pp. 17–20.

33. No byline, "Birth Control: is male contraception the answer?" *Good Housekeeping*, April 1969, vol. 168, no. 4, p. 202.

34. No byline (UPI), "Male Contraceptive Is Tested But Side-Effects Prohibit Use," *New York Times*, September 17, 1981, unpaginated clipping (Schlesinger clipping file).

35. No byline, "Researchers Test Birth Control Injection for Men," *New York Times*, February 24, 1987, unpaginated clipping (Schlesinger clipping file).

36. Sheldon J. Segal, "Contraceptive research: A male chauvinist plot?" *Family Planning Perspectives*, vol. 4, issue 3, pp. 21–25, quoted in Oudshoorn, *The Male Pill*, pp. 8–9.

37. Morton Hair, researcher at St. Mary's Hospital, University of Manchester, in an interview with the BBC News, October 25, 1998, quoted in Oudshoorn, *The Male Pill*, p. 9; Bernard Asbell, *The Pill* (New York: Random House, 1995), pp. 341–346.

38. Jane E. Brody, "Why a Lag in Male-Oriented Birth Control?" *New York Times*, October 16, 1983, p. 18 E (Schlesinger clipping file).

39. Unsigned editorial, "Men and Birth Control," *New York Times*, November 19, 1983, Section 1, page 24, Schlesinger clipping file.

40. Oudshoorn, *The Male Pill*, pp. 25–27.

41. For more on thalidomide and Kelsey, see Chapter 6.

42. Ann Banks, "Futura: The Pill for Men?" *Boston Magazine*, February 1977, p. 4, Schlesinger clipping file.

43. Erin M, age 23.

44. Quotes are from Oudshoorn, *The Male Pill*, pp. 180–181, 183, 189. For changing attitudes, see Chapter 8. For the astronaut ad, see p. 187.

45. Jonathan Bender, "244 Words on Why Men Need The Pill," *DAME for women who know better*, April 29, 2008 www.damemagazine

.com/dame-daily/features/f346/244WordsonWhyMenNeedThe Pill.php, accessed July 7, 2008.

46. Quoted in John Schieszer, "Male Birth Control Pill Soon a Reality," MSNBC at www.msnbc.msn.com/id/3543478/, accessed June 8, 2009.

47. Bender, "244 Words on Why Men Need The Pill."

48. Mary B, Internet survey respondent.

49. Stuart H, Internet survey respondent.

50. Kelly H, Internet survey respondent.

51. Cathy S, Internet survey respondent.

52. Internet survey respondents Rachel A, age 28; Donna H, age 17; Susan G, 22-year-old student.

53. MSNBC article at www.msnbc.msn.com/id/3543478/, accessed June 8, 2009.

54. BBC Web site accessed 10/4/09: http://news.bbc.co.uk/2/hi/special_report/1998/viagra/194029.stm; no byline, "Health Warnings to Viagra Users," BBC News, November 25, 1998, http://news.bbc.co.uk/2/hi/special_report/1998/viagra/221497.stm, accessed October 28, 2009.

CHAPTER 6

1. Barbara Seaman, *The Doctors' Case Against the Pill* (Alameda, CA: Hunter House, originally published 1969, 1995 edition), p. 1.

2. Elizabeth Siegel Watkins, *On the Pill: A Social History of Oral Contraceptives, 1950–1970* (Baltimore: Johns Hopkins University Press, 1998), p. 12.

3. Margaret March and Wanda Ronner, *The Fertility Doctor: John Rock and the Reproductive Revolution* (Baltimore: Johns Hopkins Univ. Press, 2008), especially Chapter 9: "The Pill Falls from Grace."

4. David Burnham, "Birth Control: End of a Taboo," *The Nation*, vol. 200, no. 4 (January 25, 1965), pp. 85–86.

5. Loretta McLaughlin, *The Pill, John Rock, and the Church: The Biography of a Revolution* (Boston: Little, Brown and Co., 1982), pp. 151–153.

6. Colin S, Internet survey respondent, October 6, 2008.

7. Quoted in *U.S. News & World Report*, vol. 55, no. 12 (September 9, 1963), p. 11.

8. Robert E. Hall, M.D., "The Church and the Pill," *The Nation*, vol. 199, no. 9 (October 5, 1964), pp. 191–193.

9. For an excellent history of the controversy within the Church and the events leading to the Pope's encyclical, see Marsh and Ronner, *The Fertility Doctor*, pp. 227–257; see also McLaughlin, *The Pill, John Rock, and the Church*.

10. For Rock's views on contraception and abortion, see Marsh and Ronner, *Fertility Doctor*, p. 241. For his Catholic upbringing, see p. 10.

11. Marsh and Ronner, *Fertility Doctor*, pp. 235–245.

12. See Rev. John W. O'Malley, *What Happened at Vatican II* (Cambridge, MA: Belknap/Harvard University Press, 2008).

13. Pete Seeger, *The Pill*, 1966.

14. Marsh and Ronner, *The Fertility Doctor*, pp. 254–255; Lara V. Marks, *Sexual Chemistry: A History of the Contraceptive Pill* (New Haven, CT: Yale University Press, 2001), Chapter 9.

15. Xavier Rynne, "Letter from Vatican City," *The New Yorker*, vol. XLIV, no. 37, November 2, 1968, pp. 131–147.

16. Marsh and Ronner, *Fertility Doctor*, pp. 227, 254.

17. Robert W. Kistner, M.D., "What 'The Pill' Does to Husbands," *Ladies Home Journal*, January 1969, pp. 66–68.

18. See, for example, David Oshinsky, *Polio: An American Story* (New York: Oxford Univ. Press, 2005); and Andrea Tone, *The Age of Anxiety: A History of America's Turbulent Affair with Tranquilizers* (New York: Basic Books, 2009).

19. Tone, *The Age of Anxiety*, p. 27, and Chapter 2 on Miltown.

20. Tone, *The Age of Anxiety*, pp. 147–150.

21. Lara V. Marks, *Sexual Chemistry: A History of the Contraceptive Pill* (New Haven, CT: Yale University Press, 2001), p. 138 and Chapter 6.

22. Aurora M, 54, African American, Internet survey respondent.

23. June S, no age given, story of her mother, Internet survey respondent.

24. Ilene W, 64, Internet survey respondent.

25. One man responding to the Internet survey recalled, "The Pill plus Barbara Seaman's book *The Doctors' Case Against the Pill* were instrumental solidifying my interest in women's health issues and becoming a pro-feminist." Stephen M, age 59, married 30 years, Canadian, Internet survey respondent.

26. Seaman, *The Doctors' Case Against the Pill*, p. 12.

27. Marsh and Ronner, *The Fertility Doctor*, pp. 269–277.

28. Marsh and Ronner, *The Fertility Doctor*, p. 275.

29. Marsh and Ronner, *The Fertility Doctor*, pp. 269–277.

30. Elizabeth Siegel Watkins, *On the Pill*, p. 4.

31. *David Susskind Show*, 1977, viewed at the Schlesinger Library. The panelists included Barbara Seaman, Melvin Taymor, M.D. (Harvard), Howard I. Shapiro, M.D. (Author of *The Birth Control Book*), Ben Zion Taber, M.D. (Stanford), and Edwin Ortiz, M.D. (FDA).

32. Tone, *Devices and Desires* (New York: Hill and Wang, 2001), p. 249.

33. Quoted in Kathy Davis, *The Making of Our Bodies, Ourselves: How Feminism Travels Across Borders* (Durham, NC: Duke University Press, 2007), p. 23.

34. Boston Women's Health Book Collective, *Our Bodies, Ourselves* (New York: Simon and Schuster, 1973 edition), p. 115.

35. BWHBC, *Our Bodies, Ourselves*, 1976 edition, p. 188; 1984 edition, p. 240, emphasis added.

36. BWHBC, *Our Bodies, Ourselves*, 1992 edition, p. 280; 1998 edition, pp. 293–294.

37. BWHBC, *Our Bodies, Ourselves, A New Edition for a New Era,* 2005, pp. 322, 332.

38. Sheldon J. Segal, *Under the Banyan Tree* (New York: Oxford University Press, 2003), pp. 95–98.

39. Quoted in Dorothy Roberts, *Killing the Black Body: Race, Reproduction, and the Meaning of Liberty* (New York: Pantheon, 1997), pp. 106–107.

40. Segal, *Under the Banyan Tree,* pp. 100–101.

41. Quoted in Roberts, *Killing the Black Body,* pp. 104–108.

42. Roberts, *Killing the Black Body,* p. 117. Dorothy Roberts also noted that distributing Norplant to adolescent girls deflected the problem away from the adult men who were largely responsible for teen pregnancies.

43. Tone, *Devices and Desires,* p. 288.

44. Segal, *Under the Banyan Tree,* pp. 101–105.

45. Segal, *Under the Banyan Tree,* p. 141.

46. More than 3,000 women sued Johnson and Johnson, claiming that users of the Ortho-Evra birth control patch suffered heart attacks and strokes. Between 2002 and 2006, the FDA received reports of fifty deaths associated with the patch. Johnson and Johnson acknowledged that the patch delivered much more estrogen than the low-dose birth control pill and that the company had not made that information available to consumers. Yet because the FDA had approved the patch and had not notified the public about potential risks until 2005, Johnson and Johnson claimed that it was not liable for any harm. New warnings were added to the package in 2006 and again in 2008. Gardiner Harris and Alex Berenson, "Drug Makers Near Old Goal: A Legal Shield," *The New York Times,* April 6, 2008, www.nytimes.com; Miranda Hitte, "Stronger Warning for Birth Control Patch: FDA Strengthens Warning on Blood Clot Risk for Users of Ortho Evra Birth Control Skin Patch," Jan. 18, 2008, WebMD Health News, reviewed by Louise Chang, M.D., www.webmd.com/sex/birth-control/news/20080118/birth-control-patch-stronger-warning, accessed 12/31/08.

47. American consumers continued to use the courts to assure product safety. In the 1990s, there were 20,000 product liability suits in the United States for all products, including contraceptives, and only 200 in the United Kingdom. Other European countries had similarly low rates of litigation. These contrasts result in part from different legal systems. For example, contingent fee arrangements, in which lawyers are paid only if they win the case for their clients, are common in the United States but not allowed in Europe. Expert witnesses in the United States are selected by each side in a conflict, leading to courtroom battles between experts who have been prepared as friendly witnesses by the lawyers whose case they promote. In Europe that practice would be considered unethical. European judges designate the experts who will testify and present scientific evidence, and lawyers cannot consult with the experts before the trial. Segal, *Under the Banyan Tree*, pp. 141–142.

48. Oudshoorn, *The Male Pill*, pp. 28–29.

CHAPTER 7

1. Susan G, 26; Carol O, 29. Unless otherwise noted, all quotes in this chapter are from respondents to the Internet survey. Notes include information provided by the respondents.

2. Anne S, 21, married, bisexual, ex-military, living below poverty line.

3. Alice Z, 30, married, white straight. She and her sisters are first-generation college attendees and first-generation birth control pill users. Atheist, Democrat. From a poor, working-class, fundamentalist Christian, small-town family. "My parents are still together but miserable."

4. Elizabeth M, 23.

5. Martha L.

6. Kelly R.

7. Jessica P, age 38, married, nonmonogamous, bisexual, a lawyer.

8. The call for stories was circulated on e-mail to numerous people who also sent it to others; it was also posted on feministing.com and linked to other sites. There were no survey questions, simply a call for people to respond with their thoughts and experiences. Although most of the respondents are women under age 40, some older women and a few men also responded. The respondents came from a wide range of racial, ethnic, and religious backgrounds, marital status, and sexual orientations.

9. Melissa G.

10. Samantha J, 23.

11. Jessica P, age 38, married, nonmonogamous, bisexual, lawyer.

12. Karen E, 21, bisexual, living with boyfriend for 3 yrs.

13. http://www.thepill.com/thepill/shared/pi/Tri-Cyclen_Lo_PI.pdf#zoom=100, accessed 1/1/09.

14. http://www.webmd.com/sex/birth-control/birth-control-pill, accessed 1/1/09; http://kidshealth.org/teen/sexual_health/contraception/contraception_birth.html, accessed 1/1/09.

15. http://www.epigee.org/guide/pill_sex.html, accessed 1/1/09.

16. Mandy B.

17. Helen P, 20.

18. Valerie J, 24.

19. Barbara E, married.

20. Sally G, 27.

21. Caroline Tiger, "10 myths about the pill busted," CNN Web site, March 13, 2007, http://www.cnn.com/2007/HEALTH/03/13/healthmag.pill/index.html.

22. Susan G, 26, chemical engineer, divorced, now living with her partner.

23. Katie M, 22, white, grad student, bisexual, single.

24. Jenny B, age 31, married, bisexual, began pill at 15, from a small town in north Florida.

25. Kristy H, 23.

26. Melissa B, 26.

27. Carrie R, 20, student, Canada.

28. Linda L, 27, white, pharmacy tech.

29. Erika B.

30. Carolyn P, 20.

31. Anita K, 25.

32. Julie D, 29.

33. Jane B, Melissa G, Carol O, 29.

34. Kristol R, 29.

35. As researcher Sheldon Segal explained regarding the placebo phase of the pill, "This schedule was not a medical requirement, but a marketing decision based on the belief that women consider menstruation as natural, and would be reluctant to use a product that stopped their periods." With the newly formulated pills, "Finally, women will be freed from the control of marketers who decided that women want to have a pseudo-menstruation every month. They'll be able to decide themselves." Segal, *Under the Banyan Tree*, p. 78.

36. Robyn E, 22, Oxford, England.

37. Mary M, 23.

38. Linda O, 20.

39. Letty C, 27.

40. Jane D.

41. Natasha Singer, "A Birth Control Pill That Offered Too Much," *New York Times*, Feb. 11, 2009, www.nytimes.com/2009/02/11/business/11pill.html?_r=1&hp.

42. Lauren C, 23.

43. Renae J, 20.

44. Lucy T, Canadian, 20, student, single.

45. Regina H.

46. Marianne B.

47. Lorena A, age 20.

48. Lynn E, 34, librarian, white, married 7 years to first boyfriend, only sex partner.

49. Cassie K, 24.

50. Shelley H, 27.

51. Alissa A, age 28, married six years, liberal, college graduate, sexually active since age 18.

52. Sue G, 22.

53. Mandy B, 26.

54. Kendra H, 23.

55. Jacqueline G, writer and executive producer, married.

56. Rose H, 27.

57. Anita B, 26, graduate student.

58. "National Conference of State Legislators Pharmacist Conscience Clauses: Laws and Legislation," www.ncsl.org/Default.aspx? TabId=14380, updated May 2009; Saundra Young, "White House set to reverse health care conscience clause," www.cnn.com/2009/ POLITICS/02/27/conscience.rollback/index.html 2/27/09CNN.

59. Katie M, 22-year-old white graduate student from Indiana, nondenominational Christian, bisexual, single.

60. Krista A, 34, graduate student in medical science, married.

61. Amy K, age 25, Midwestern, married, feminist.

62. Ricardo Alonso-Zaldivar, "FDA to allow 'morning-after' pill for 17-year-olds," Associated Press, April 23, 2009; baltimoresun.com 4/25/09, "The politics of Plan B: Our view: Morning-after pill for teens is safe, but no substitute for doctor's care"; Marc Kaufman, "Nonprescription Sale Sought for Contraceptive; Petition to FDA to Offer 'Morning After' Pill Over the Counter Could Become Entangled in Abortion Debate," *Washington Post,* April 21, p. A02; Susan Aschoff, "In Case of Emergency Break Glass: Birth Control Has Backup," *St. Petersburg Times* (Florida), April 09, 2002, South Pinellas Edition, p. 3D.

63. Krista A, 34, grad student in medical science, married.

64. Cathy P, 20.

CONCLUSION

1. "The Age of the Thing," *The Economist,* December 25, 1993, Section Modern Wonders, p. 47 (U.K. Edition, p. 87).

2. Quote and data from Sheldon J. Segal, *Under the Banyan Tree* (New York: Oxford University Press, 2003), p. 77.

3. William D. Mosher, Ph.D.; Gladys M. Martinez, Ph.D.; Anjani Chandra, Ph.D.; Joyce C. Abma, Ph.D.; and Stephanie J. Wilson, Ph.D., Division of Vital Statistics, "Use of Contraception and Use of Family Planning Services in the United States: 1982–2002," *Advance Data From Vital and Health Statistics,* Department of Health and Human Services, Number 350, December 10, 2004.

4. Judy G, 23, Internet survey respondent.

5. In 2002, 7 percent of single women whose partners used condoms also used the pill, although double protection was much less common among married women. See Mosher et al., "Use of Contraception."

6. Boston Women's Health Book Collective, *Our Bodies, Ourselves* (New York: Touchstone, 2005 edition), pp. 332, 347.

7. Andrea Tone, *Devices and Desires* (New York: Hill and Wang, 2001), pp. 203, 233–236.

INDEX